Landscapes of
ALGARVE

a countryside guide
Eighth edition

Brian and Eileen Anderson

SUNFLOWER BOOKS

For Kate and the late Deric Brown

Eighth edition © **2017**
Sunflower Books™
PO Box 36160
London SW7 3WS, UK
www.sunflowerbooks.co.uk

ISBN 978-1-85691-491-8

Almond tree letter box

Important note to the reader

We have tried to ensure that the descriptions and maps in this book are
error-free at press date. The book will be updated, where necessary,
whenever future printings permit. It will be very helpful for us to receive
your comments (sent in care of the publishers, please) for the updating
of future printings, and for the Update service described on the inside
back cover of the book.

We also rely on those who use this book — especially walkers — to
take along a good supply of common sense when they explore.
Conditions change fairly rapidly in Algarve, and *storm damage or
bulldozing may make a route unsafe at any time*. If the route is not as we
outline it here, and your way ahead is not secure, return to the point of
departure. *Never attempt to complete a tour or walk under hazardous
conditions!* Please read carefully the notes on pages 38 to 47, as well as
the introductory comments at the beginning of each tour and walk
(regarding road conditions, equipment, grade, distances and time, etc).
Explore *safely* while at the same time respecting the beauty of the
countryside.

Cover photograph: Ponta da Piedade (Walk 1)
Title page: Tiles (azulejos) in Largo 1 de Dezembro, Portimão

Photographs: the authors, except for the cover (Shutterstock)
Maps: Nick Hill for Sunflower Books. Base map data © OpenStreetMap
   contributors. Contour data made available under ODbL (opendata
   commons.org/licenses/odbl/1.0)
A CIP catalogue record for this book is available from the British Library.
Printed and bound in the UK: Short Run Press, Exeter

Contents

4   Landscapes of Algarve

Falésia, near Vilamoura

Preface

Legend tells of how a Moorish king married a Scandinavian beauty and brought her to Algarve. She loved to watch the sun's rays seeking out and painting the hilltops in hues of evening gold. But when the summer season faded through autumn into winter, she became deeply unhappy and pined longingly for the snows of her native land. Worried at the unhappy state of his beloved, the king arranged for thousands and thousands of almond trees to be planted throughout the region. Even now, in January and February, the land is dusted with a covering of almond blossom in delicate shades of pink and white lying like a soft fall of snow, filling the hollows and outlining the hillsides.

Below the 'snow' lies a carpet of burnished gold, as the Bermuda buttercups burst into bloom to announce the arrival of spring. Oranges fill the trees; iris, bluebells, and even the insect-mimicking wild orchids follow in abundance. 'Is this the same Algarve', you may ask, 'as the Algarve of high-rise hotels, fine beaches and a coastline so famous that there is no need to look further?' Such is the beauty of the coastline, that few visitors look for more — but we did. We found a countryside full of interest and beauty, quietly awaiting discovery. From flowers and fountains, hilltops and history, to windmills and watermills, we can set your feet wandering to find them all. There are car tours, too, to get you out and about, searching out little-known points of interest — like the huge rose compass *(rosa dos ventos)* on the barren promontory of Sagres, where Prince Henry the Navigator founded his school of navigation, or the Moorish castle and old Roman bridge at Paderne.

But don't think for one moment that we have turned our backs on and ignored the beautiful and rugged western coastline. Wherever it is still unspoilt and free from development, we have incorporated it into a walk. Some of the finest and most picturesque coastline in Algarve is yours to share only with others who are happy to tread the coastal paths. There are quieter bays, too, where you can take a break from walking, for a relaxing dip in the sea and perhaps a refreshing glass of well-chilled *vinho verde* before stepping out to complete the walk.

Some days are made for relaxing, so why not try a country picnic? We have highlighted a variety of picnic suggestions at the top of the relevant car tours and walks, many involving only a short walk. Some are set in country villages — like the one at Alte, which gives you a chance to explore an old settlement and enjoy a short stroll by the riverside, before settling down to your picnic lunch. Or perhaps you feel ready for the hustle and bustle of a country market. Here you can feel the excitement of the locals, share the life, the colour, the customs and culture for a few short hours before it all fades to empty stalls.

However you like to spend your holidays, Algarve offers something for everybody. If you like lively resorts or quiet resorts, you'll find them but, best of all, with the help of this book, you can easily escape the crowds. Step out with us and share our delight at finding tranquillity and undreamed-of countryside — in the very heart of Algarve.

Acknowledgements

In particular, we would like to thank our late good friend Deric Brown of Vila da Luz for the Figueira circuit (Walk 4) and for general on-the-spot checks and suggestions; all the users of the book who send in constructive comments; 'hotter' (tel 0800-468837), who supplied Eileen with the most comfortable pair of light walking boots she has ever worn, ideally suited to Algarve walking, and our ever-patient publisher, Pat Underwood.

Background reading

Visitors Guide *Algarve*, by the same authors, on Kindle. For a deeper insight into the Algarvian way of life, track down *Southern Portugal; its people, traditions and wildlife* by John and Madge Measures (published in Algarve and on sale locally).

Praia Dona Ana (near the end of Walk 1)

Getting about

With so much interest focused on the coastal zone, it is not surprising to find this region is well served by public transport. **Buses** ply back and forth along the main highway, the N125, calling in at the various coastal towns. All the services are timetabled and generally keep good time. It always pays to arrive a few minutes earlier for the bus than the scheduled time. A selection of useful timetables for the EVA bus company (www.eva-bus.com) is given in the timetable section on pages 131-133, but *do* check up-to-date times on their website. The Frota Azul bus company operates in the west (www.frotazul-algarve.pt); many timestables are downloadable.

There is a very useful **train service** which runs almost the length of Algarve, from Lagos in the west to Vila Real on the eastern border. With 45 stations along this line, it can be a slow journey — taking as long as four and a half hours to travel the whole length, but it is much cheaper than the buses. The full timetable is too long and detailed to include in our timetables, but a short extract is given, which might be useful for getting to the start of some of the walks. Full timetables are available free of charge from most stations, some tourist offices, and at www.cp.pt.

Taxis are plentiful in the main tourist resorts, and these are especially useful for getting out to some of the more remote regions, but we would advise you only to use official taxis. Meters are not commonly in use, so it is wise to enquire about the fare before you start the journey. In our limited experience, we found that the taxi drivers were fairly consistent in applying the fares, and that we were paying the same rates as the local people. If you can team up with other walkers to reduce the cost, then taxis represent a very convenient way of getting out into the countryside from the main centres but, in most cases, you would need to arrange to be collected to get back again.

The limitations of the public transport system are only fully realised when you want to get to the inland villages and countryside — which you will need to do for many of our walks. This is where a **hire car** is invaluable. See the notes on pages 10-13 about car hire and driving. *All* of the walks are suitable for motorists, and we give you way-points for the walk start so that you can set your satnav.

☀ Picnicking

Beaches are popular venues for picnics in Algarve, but there are many lovely and more tranquil country settings. It is not unusual to find small picnic areas as you drive around. These are usually sited amongst trees, with wooden or stone tables and benches.

We have chosen a variety of picnic settings that we particularly enjoy, and have highlighted them in the headings of the car tours and walks. Some lie deep in the countryside, others on secluded beaches (but remember that in mid-summer *all* beaches are fairly busy). Most of these picnic spots are easily accessible; a few, due to their isolation, require more walking — but they make great leg-stretchers and are well worth the extra effort involved.

If the picnic setting is on the route of a car tour, it is mentioned in the touring notes as 'PTM', to indicate that the location is shown by a P symbol on the *touring map*. No further explanation is necessary, as you can drive to the picnic spot. But if the picnic is on the route of a walk, it is highlighted in the car touring notes by the symbol P followed by the relevant walk number. The exact location of the picnic spot is then shown on a large-scale *walking map*, and a 🚗 symbol indicates the nearest parking place. If any walking is involved, the notes for the accompanying walk will tell you how to get there. Quite a few of the picnic settings are illustrated — to inspire you!

Please remember that if more than a few minutes' walking is required, you will need to wear **sensible shoes** and to take a **sunhat** (some picnic spots are **in full sun**). **Beach towels** will come in handy on sand or prickly terrain — maybe with something waterproof underneath early in the season when the ground might still be damp.

Picnic food suggestions are not much of a problem in Algarve, with well-stocked modern supermarkets. Portimão, Albufeira, Faro and Olhão also boast large supermarkets with their own bakeries and butchers, where you can buy fresh bread, even on a Sunday. Locate the local bakery for a wide choice of fresh bread: *pão seco* (small bread rolls) are ideal for picnics. From the local market buy fresh *pepino* (cucumber), *tomates* (tomatoes), *alface* (lettuce), *pimentos* (peppers), *azeitonas* (olives: *verdes* = green, *pretas* = black), *iogurte* (yogurt), *mel* (honey), *queijo* *fresco* (very mild fresh goat's cheese), and plenty of seasonal fresh fruit. There is a good variety of cheeses, cheese slices and portions.

Portuguese specialities, available ready-made from the delicatessen counter, include *rissois* (rissoles) and croquettes. There is a choice of cooked meats and sausages. *Carne* = meat, usually *porco* (pork) or *carneiro* (lamb). *Peru* (turkey) and *frango* (chicken) are also popular. We also discovered small tins of sardine pâté, ideal for picnics ... but be careful not to buy the 'piquant' variety, unless you like it hot. There are varied *bolos* (cakes), since cake and coffee play an important part in everyday Portuguese life. Food signs are not usually in English, so it helps to have a phrase-book handy.

Last, but not least, don't forget something to drink. There is a wide range of soft drinks including fruit juice, flavoured yogurt drinks, and bottled water. For more heady refreshment, take a bottle of *vinho* (wine). Portugal offers a wide range of wines, and an enjoyable element of your holiday will probably be trying many of them. *Vinho verde* ('green wine', but usually white and slightly sparkling) is an excellent choice for picnics, but a rosé or light fruity red would be equally acceptable. *Saúde!*

Restored but sail-less windmill at the 38min-point in Walk 16

❀ Touring

Algarve is a fascinating region to explore, offering a varied choice of landscapes. Sometimes relatively short distances can take a long time to cover, due to the winding nature of the roads. But travel across much of the region is easy, due to good roads and the A22 motorway*.

Although there is a good bus and train service along the coast, it is difficult to reach inland areas easily. Hiring a car gives you the freedom to see and savour the varied countryside at your own pace, as well as allowing forays off the beaten track. The rural road network in Algarve is very variable — from very good to virtually impassable, all probably taking longer to drive than you may anticipate.

Our pull-out touring map is ideal for planning and in fact contains all the information you will need outside the towns. There is a fairly wide selection of **touring maps**, but old editions are often mixed in with the new, *so check the date before buying!*

Car hire is inexpensive out of the main season (April to October). It is preferable to stay with the well-known hire companies, through whom you can arrange and pay for hire before you leave, including all taxes, CDW, and unlimited mileage. There are also very reasonable fly-drive offers, especially outside the main tourist season.

Take care when renting; check the car and take time to study the **rental conditions/insurance coverage**. It is imperative to ensure that 'collision damage waiver' is included in the insurance, to cover damage to your hire car if repair costs cannot be recovered from a third party. Tyre and windscreen damage (including punctures) are the responsibility of the hirer, so check carefully before you drive off, including the spare. Always carry the agency's phone number with you, and take some water, food, and warm clothing in case of breakdown.

Since the DVLC has withdrawn the paper part of UK drivers' licenses containing information on penalty points/

*An **electronic toll system** operates on the A22: there are *no* manned toll booths. All car rental firms will explain the procedure to you, and most rental cars come equipped with an electronic gadget called a 'transponder', pre-loaded with credits. You can top up the credits at any time, or have the cost deducted from your hire charges if you know in advance that you will never use the A22. To read more about this system (which is likely to catch on in other countries), see www.portugaltolls.com.

driving convictions, it's a good idea to know how to obtain an 'access code' if you intend to hire a car in Portugal. The code will allow the car hire company to inspect this information online on the DVLC website. You can get your personal code from the DVLC website by entering your driving license and National Insurance numbers. But note that the code is only valid for 21 days.

The wearing of **seat belts** is compulsory, and locals comply outside the main towns, but there seems to be some unspoken agreement that they aren't necessary in built-up areas. Always wear your seat belt! Rear seat belts must also be worn, and children under 13 are not allowed as front seat passengers.

Petrol stations are frequent along the N125, and many of them are open seven days a week; some of the international companies offer a 24-hour service. There are fewer petrol stations in country areas, and many are closed on Sunday. If you are heading inland, go with a full tank of petrol. Some grades of petrol may be unfamiliar: *super* is self-explanatory, as is *diesel*, but *sem chumbo* = unleaded. A petrol station by the roundabout at the entrance to Faro airport is convenient for those returning hire cars.

Drive carefully: the road is regarded as a walkway, especially in country areas. Be extra vigilant for animals and the occasional large-wheeled cart still encountered in the country. Be aware also that even main roads almost invariably narrow appreciably where they cross bridges and sometimes where they pass through small villages; there are usually no warnings.

There has been a vast improvement in the **standard of driving**, but be wary — particularly with regard to overtaking. The N125 along the coast is still treated as a motorway by some locals. It is mainly a single-lane flow, with an additional lane at the side for breakdowns and very slow moving traffic like farm tractors. In some places there are short, well signposted stretches, expressly for overtaking.

The significance of **zebra crossings** is confusing, as there are no beacons to indicate their presence, but they are generally respected. Many traffic lights and junctions have been replaced by **roundabouts** *(rotundas)*. **Road markings** have also been greatly improved in recent years.

There are frequent **police checks**, so it is essential for the driver to have the relevant documents relating to the vehicle, driving licence and passport to hand if a heavy fine is to be avoided.

Remember to take a **pocket phrase-book**, if only for

the road signs; you won't find them written in English. A parking sign depicting what looks like a comb and a car = park at an angle to the road to maximise parking space; *perigo* = danger; *desvio* = diversion; *lombas* = a ridge in the road to slow traffic. (The intriguing 'Património do Estado' engraved on many buildings and monuments simply translates to 'government property'.)

Telephones are widely available, but only take phone cards; otherwise hotels, restaurants, bars and shops will let you use their phones (but check the unit rates first). Remember that **mobiles** can incur hefty roaming charges abroad and that using mobiles while driving in Portugal can result in a fine.

WCs are available in most towns — in market halls, supermarkets, bus and railway stations, restaurants, cafes and some petrol stations. Don't always rely on toilet paper being supplied; carry your own.

The **touring notes** are brief: they include little history or information about the towns. Some literature is available from tourist offices, and sometimes we refer you to the walking notes for more comment but, for more information, see our background reading list on page 6. We concentrate mainly on the 'logistics' of touring: times and distances, road conditions, viewpoints and good places to rest. Most of all we emphasise possibilities for **walking** and **picnicking**; for information about the picnic spots highlighted in the notes, see page 8. If you want to stretch your legs, look at the short walks listed with the main walks. This should give you a taste of the landscapes, sufficient to whet your appetite for more.

There are many centres of tourism along the coast of Algarve, all of which can easily be keyed into the routes of the car tours from our chosen starting points. Three of the tours start in the east, from Faro, and two in the west, from the Lagôa roundabout on the N125.

Allow plenty of time for **stops**: our times include only short breaks at viewpoints labelled (☞) in the touring notes. Distances quoted are *cumulative km* from Faro or the Lagôa roundabout. A key to the symbols in the notes is on the touring map.

If you only hire a car for one day, Tour 1, a long trip, provides a sampler, encompassing the windswept coast and the pastoral serenity of the Serra de Monchique. If you don't wish to drive quite as far, Tour 3 takes you through an appealing and gentler countryside, punctuated by the intriguing *rochas* of Pena and Soidos. Most of our hire cars recorded whole kilometres only, so our distances are not always accurate to the nearest decimal place, which left us guessing a little at some distances below a kilometre. This shouldn't cause any problems when used in conjunction with the other instructions.

All motorists should read the country code on page 44 and go quietly in the countryside.

Grilling sardines at an outdoor restaurant in Portimão

COUNTRY FAIRS AND MARKETS

Market day is a day of great atmosphere and excitement for the local people. It is a chance to look for bargains, shop for locally-grown produce, buy goods that are not normally available in the local shops, or even sell or buy some livestock. Just about everything is on offer at some of the larger markets, and it is particularly those with a livestock section that are best described as 'country fairs'. Here temporary bars and eating places are set up, where the menfolk seal most of their bargains.

None of this is window-dressing for tourism, so here is an opportunity to see at first hand the ordinary life of the local people, to observe and appreciate their customs. It is a snapshot on life. You might also be tempted to buy; some of the home-produced honey is good value, as is bedding and towelling. If you feel like a snack while you are walking around, try the *farturas,* which look like doughnut rings — but make sure they are hot.

The markets are held on a regular timetable, most taking place monthly.

Weekly markets

Saturdays: Loulé, São Brás   Wednesdays: Quarteira

Fortnightly market

Tuesdays (1st and 3rd in the month): Albufeira

Monthly markets

1st Sunday: Moncarapacho	1st Monday: Portimão
1st Friday: Sagres	1st Saturday: Lagos
2nd Sunday: Estói*	2nd Monday: Algoz*
3rd Monday: Silves	3rd Thursday: Alte
4th Saturday: Tunes	4th Monday: Messines

*These are two of the bigger markets — really country fairs

Car tour 1: THE WEST COAST TOUR

Lagôa • Portimão • Lagos • Sagres • Aljezur • Marmelete • Silves • Lagôa

201km/125mi; about 4 hours' driving: start from the Lagôa roundabout, on the N125, heading west towards Portimão.

Walks en route: 1-5, 7-11; Walks 6 and 12 are a short detour away

Picnic suggestions: Luz obelisk (*P*1), Ponta da Almádena (*P*3), Boca do Rio (*P*3), Zavial or Ingrina beach (*P*4), Silves windmill (*P*11), Bravura reservoir (*P*TM), Caldas de Monchique (*P*TM); Marinha and Albandeira beaches are nearby (*P*12)

On the whole, all the roads are well surfaced.

Visit the pleasant resort of Lagos and enjoy a spectacular coastline which still harbours a few relatively unspoilt fishing villages. Windswept Sagres, one-time home of Prince Henry the Navigator, is now a favoured spot for fishermen who hang precariously from the rocky cliffs at dizzy heights. Follow the Atlantic coast northwards, past deserted sandy beaches. Visit the castle at Aljezur, before turning inland to yet more dramatic scenery, as you head towards the highest mountain range in Algarve.

Starting from the roundabout at **Lagôa** on the N125, head west towards Portimão. Pass a left turn to a 'water slide' park and keep ahead on the N125 (or use the A22 to go directly to Lagos). Take the next right turn (5km) to Portimão. The road leads back under the N125 and into town over the old narrow bridge. Turn left immediately on crossing the bridge and head for the centre of **Portimão** (10km ⛺🏨✕🛒⊕🏖WC). To park, keep heading south in the one-way system and, once beyond the centre, follow signs left to Faro. This leads you back along the river, where you can park. (To continue directly to Lagos from here, head back to the old bridge. Don't cross the bridge; turn left and follow signs to Lagos, to rejoin the N125.)

From Portimão head south, parallel with the river, to **Praia da Rocha** (13km ⛺🏨✕🏖). A left turn at the promenade leads to the remains of the 16th-century fort of Santa Catarina which guarded the mouth of the River Arade, once navigable to Silves. Now the fort provides a good viewpoint across the river to Ferragudo and the 17th-century fort of São João. Now follow the coast road west to **Vau** and on to the old fishing village of **Alvor** (18km). Then the road swings inland to the N125 at the end of the Portimão bypass (21.5km). Turn left through pleasant countryside. After 4km you pass 100m to the left of the railway station at **Mexilhoeira Grande**, where Walk 5 begins and ends. At **Odiáxere** (29km) the road narrows; in the village centre, you could turn right to the Barragem

14

da Bravura (⊚✕*P*TM). The bridge over the Ribeira de Bensafrim is swiftly crossed. Turn left at the roundabout to head into the shimmering white town of **Lagos★** (34km ⍭✝▲▲✕⌷△⌷M WC). Drive alongside the river to find car parks and plenty of parking on the roadside.

From Lagos stay with the riverside road/N125, which sweeps up past the fort and round the back of Lagos; follow signs for Luz/Sagres. (Ponta da Piedade, Porto de Mós and Praia Dona Ana, settings for Walk 1, are signposted off left.) Keep ahead at the roundabout, where a right turn heads back to Faro. The pretty, gently undulating countryside along this next stretch of road is very appealing. Pass the turn-off to Luz (✝▲▲✕△⌷WC*P*1; Walks 1 and 2) in 45km; the village is 3km down the road to the left. Under 3km from the Luz road, at traffic lights (48km), you pass a road right into Espiche and 'Zoo'. (This road leads to Walk 6: keep following 'Zoo' and 'Barão de São João', to reach Barão de São João after some 6km.)

Ignoring the 'Zoo' turning, once past **Espiche** notice the left turn to Burgau★ (53km; ▲✕⌷WC; Walk 3). Burgau is 2km down the road, and Ponta da Almádena (*P*3) a further 2km west from there. *Matos*-covered rolling hills with pockets of cultivation lie beyond the tree-lined road. This takes on a wilder aspect once you pass **Vale de Boi** (51km). Soon after **Budens** (56.5km ⍭) watch for a left turn (52.5km) signposted to Salema. This turn-off leads to both Figueira (Walk 4) and Salema★ (▲▲✕⌷ WC*P*3; Walk 3).

There are fewer signs of habitation here, as the *matos,* now becoming stunted due to the windswept location, invades the countryside. After passing the Salema turn-off, turn right on the old road for 'Guadalupe'. This leads to the chapel of Nossa Senhora de Guadalupe, where Henry the Navigator is thought to have worshipped. The old road soon rejoins the N125. At **Raposeira** (64km) a left turn at the traffic lights gives access to the beaches of Zavial and Ingrina (△*P*4). Around here large tracts of pastureland dominate the scenery. This gives way to green and well-farmed, gently-rolling hills as you approach **Vila do Bispo** (66km ✝✕), where you keep round left towards Sagres on the main N268. An obvious absence of trees, except for those lining the road, confirms the windswept, wild nature of this narrow strip of land jutting out into the Atlantic.

As you approach a roundabout (75km), a fort fills in the landscape. Keep ahead to visit the **Fortaleza de Sagres** (76km). Inside, there is a huge pebble wind-compass (*rosa*

BORDEIRA — *Circular walk for motorists* (● *14km; 3h30min-5h*)

This route leads through a valley once filled with paddy fields. Yes! Algarve was once a rice-growing area. The concrete towers, spread at intervals along the main track through the valley, appear to have been sluice gates to control the water flow. You rise through *matos*-covered hills to the high point at the hamlet of Monte Novo, then relish magnificent views along the west coast and an abundance of spring flowers on the return.

All on tracks, this walk can be shortened to about 6km. After an initial short uphill section, there is a gradual rise to the hamlet of Monte Novo, the halfway point. Beyond there, two short stretches of woodland *provide the only shade en route*. Four information boards, the first at the start, punctuate the way *(but don't rely on them!)*. Carry water and a picnic; there are no refreshments en route. An excellent **free map and gps track** can be downloaded from the WIP website (see panel on page 39): download 'Alj PR20'.

Start out in the lay-by, by BOARD NO 1. Head northwest down the track opposite the Bordeira road. In under a minute, fork right to cross a concrete ford. Turn left uphill at the track junction (**5min**) then downhill right, into the valley, at the next junction (**14min**). You may have to climb over some

---

dos ventos), a chapel, a café and an indifferent museum. You can also walk out to the lighthouse at the end of the promontory (☎). Return to the roundabout and turn right into **Sagres★** (▲▲✕🅿🛒). The square on the right has pleasant cafés; it's 1km further down to the fishing harbour.

Head back to the roundabout to continue to Cape St Vincent on a straight road through low scrub — but save your visit for another day if a gale is blowing! The elements may have tried to subdue growth in this corner of Algarve, but the botanist may well be surprised at the variety of flora awaiting discovery among the cowering bushes. You pass another fort on the left just before the lighthouse, the **Fortaleza de Beliche** (84km ✕). The position of the lighthouse, 9° west of Greenwich, makes **Cabo de São Vicente** (80km) one of the most westerly points in Europe. The long-distance Algarve Way ends here.

Retrace your route back to **Vila do Bispo** (101km) and turn right to loop over the road (signposted for Aljezur and Lisbon). The tree-lined N268 now runs parallel with the coast through softer, more undulating terrain. From **Carrapateira** (115km 🛒), an isolated spot, roads lead off left to mainly-deserted sandy beaches. Pockets of green cultivation make patterns among the *matos*-covered low hills. As you approach **Bordeira**, the circular walk in the panel above leaves from a large lay-by on the left (119km).

When you meet the main Lagos/Lisbon road (N120; 129km), turn left. As you approach Aljezur you will see the castle on the hill above the town. Drive through **Aljezur** (135km 🏧🛍▲✕🅿☎🛒WC), where the main road sweeps round right and over a bridge. Park on the left, just

cattle-restraining wires here. If the deep pool, where a winter stream crosses, is full of water, stay on the right-hand side and cross on some stones sunk into the mud. When you meet a crossing track by a CONCRETE TOWER with iron rungs on the left (**28min**), turn right. *(But go left for the short 6km circuit.)*

At the T-junction (**34min**) turn left, to BOARD NO 2. Rise towards Monte Novo, and keep left where another track continues ahead to the farmhouse at MONTE VELHO (**1h07min**). Now on the waymarked Ruta Vincentina, pass an isolated building on the left and continue to BOARD NO 3 at the entrance to **Monte Novo**. Wind through the hamlet to the left, and leave on the track signed to MALHADAS DE CERVA, following electricity poles. Views open up along the west coast, and the flowers in spring are wonderful.

A gradual descent leads south to BOARD NO 4 (**2h09min**). Ten minutes later a track leads right to a trig point. Descend to a 5-WAY JUNCTION, with a large threshing floor on the left, possibly used for rice and cereals. *(The short circuit enters from the left here.)* Stay ahead, skirting to the left of farm buildings above right (**2h46min**) and passing two smaller threshing floors. At a staggered junction (**3h**), keep round to the left. Cross a river ford and ignore a track off right. Keep ahead past fields on the left, back to BOARD NO 1.

---

over the bridge, by the tourist office. To walk up to the castle (10 minutes), cross back over the river on a foot-bridge, to a small square. With your back to the river, take the cobbled road up from the far right-hand corner of the square and continue round to the left, to climb through old Aljezur. Then take the track up left to the castle. Little remains except for the walls, a vaulted cistern and two towers. But the castle is an excellent viewpoint: looking inland, Fóia, the highest peak in Algarve and the setting for Walk 8, can be spotted in the distance.

Leave the car park and turn left towards Lisbon; almost immediately there is a junction, where you go right on the N267 towards Marmelete and Monchique. *(But first you might like to continue north on the N120 to the Rogil Nature Reserve for the short walk in the panel overleaf.)* The N267 is a spectacular high-level road (📷) which crosses a narrow ridge where valleys plunge down steeply on either side. Pretty hollows of cultivation and rolling hills — a carpet of white flowers in spring — catch the eye.

As you start to descend (147.5km) there are glimpses of the Barragem da Bravura not too far to the right (📷). Fóia, the highest point, distinguished by its cluster of antennae, can also be seen ahead. Beyond **Marmelete** (151km 🍴🅿), woodland softens and cloaks the landscape, as the left turn to Chilrão (157km; Walk 7) is passed. On the approach to **Casais** (160km) the trees screening the roadside part to reveal views to the right. Then, suddenly, as you penetrate further into the **Serra de Monchique**, the scene changes yet again, as deep terraced valleys create an alpine picture (📷).

ROGIL NATURE RESERVE — *Short walk for motorists* ●

This is an easy and delightful short walk of 2.5km (1h) through sand dunes, which are home to a variety of coastal flora. Tread carefully!

From Aljezur, continue north on the N120, drive to the far end of Rogil and turn left to Esteveira. Park in the open area on the right after 3.2km, where the road ends. From the car park walk left, seawards, along the track between two red-roofed white houses. Where the track becomes sandy (4min), fork left on a path. There are a few sandy paths: just head south along the cliff top. In around 30min, the path swings inland, with a gully over to the right and pines on the left. Continue circling left, edging the pine wood, until the car park comes into view ahead. Do not walk across the fields, but stay on the path which heads right, back to the track, just before the houses met on the way out. Turn right, back to the car park.

Turn right downhill towards Portimão on reaching the main road at **Nave** (N266; 164km).* In 3km you pass the **Miradouro das Caldas** (✕⌂▣) on the right — a good viewpoint over Caldas de Monchique. Continue to wind downhill and, if you have time to visit the shady ancient spa of Caldas★ (▲⌂✕▣⌂♨WC*P*TM; Car tour 2), a right turn in a little over 1km is the only vehicular access into the centre. But it is difficult from this approach — an acutely-angled turn back the way you came. It's easier to park at the roundabout 400m ahead (168km): turn right here and park at the *end* of the one-way system through Caldas, leaving a five-minute walk to the centre.

Once down from the hills (174.5km), the wooded areas are left behind, and the road straightens out as it heads towards Portimão. At the **Porto de Lagos** roundabout (180.5km), turn left for Silves on the N124. (Or, for a quicker return to Lagôa, keep ahead to join the A22 on the outskirts of Portimão and turn left towards Faro.) Enjoy some tranquil scenery as you drive along this road, passing Walk 10 en route, to **Silves★** (191.5km ▮♦ ▲✕▣⊕⌂M♨WC*P*11; Walk 11; Car tour 2). If you wish to stop in Silves, which is up to the left, park in the car park on the right or alongside the road skirting the town. See Walk 11 for more details.

Continue back to Lagôa by turning right over the river below Silves (193km), and then turn right again. This leads you back onto the N125, where you can turn left, back to the **Lagôa roundabout** (201km).

*A left turn would take you up to Monchique★ (♦⌂✕▣⊕♨WC; Walks 9-11). See Car tour 2 for more details about Monchique.

Car tour 2: MOUNTAINS AND 'MOORS'

Lagôa • Silves • Caldas de Monchique • Monchique • Fóia • Lagôa

91km/57mi; about 2 hours' driving: start from Lagôa roundabout, on the main N125, and head north to Silves.

Walks en route: 7-11

Picnic suggestions: Silves windmill (*P*11), Caldas de Monchique (*P*TM); the Arade reservoir (*P*TM) is nearby

The road up from Monchique to Fóia is narrow, but wide enough for two cars. If possible, save this tour for a day when you can see the Serra de Monchique clearly from Lagôa, so that you will be able fully to appreciate the superb views.

Highlights on this memorable tour include the imposing remains at Silves — the Moors' capital of Algarve, an ancient spa set amidst soft green foliage and recalling days gone by, and the breathtaking views from the highest point in the tour, Fóia.

From **Lagôa** (✝⌂✕☎⬛) head west on the N125. At the A22 access roundabout, turn inland towards the motorway (Junction 6) and follow signs to Silves. There are good views of the castle on the descent (📷) towards **Silves★** (⛨✝⌂✕☎⊕☂Ⓜ WC*P*11; Walk 11). The castle ramparts glow red in early morning or evening sunlight. Turn left over the river and left again at the T-junction (7.5km).* There is a large car park and tourist office further along the riverside on the left (as well as limited parking and a smaller car park on the right). See the notes with Walk 11 (page 80) for more information about Silves and to guide you up to the town centre — and to the windmill, if you would like to picnic there. Besides the interesting historical remains and a museum, the daily market in Silves, almost opposite the old bridge, is excellent for fresh produce.

Leave Silves and continue west towards Monchique. Some 4km from Silves roundabout, you pass the Mira-Rio restaurant on the left, where Walk 10 begins. A winding road now leads through pretty pastoral countryside, where oranges and lemons grow in abundance. This is a major orange-growing area, and en route to Monchique you will pass many roadside stalls selling oranges.

Meet a roundabout after 18.5km and turn right on the N266 towards Monchique and the mountains. A mass of purple from the many Judas trees lining the road here brings a splash of colour in spring. Enjoy a pleasant drive

---

*A right turn at this T-junction leads in the direction of São Bartolomeu de Messines and the Barragem do Arade (✕*P*TM). This road passes the 'Cruz de Portugal', a 16th-century cross which is set on the left just past the next exit from Silves.

Once the capital of Algarve, Silves is now an orange-growing centre and a pleasant place to take a break (Car tours 1 and 2, Walk 11).

towards the foothills of the distinctive Serra de Monchique, past cultivated fields and through scattered hamlets. Fields give way to woodland as the road starts to wind and twist uphill (24.5km). This is a beautiful climb on days when the sun filtering through the trees casts dancing, shimmering shadows. Pass a very large shady lay-by on the right (28km), before reaching the roundabout exit from Caldas de Monchique on the left (29km). This is the entrance to the spa hotel and the water bottling plant, but the exit from the one-way system through Caldas itself. It is possible to turn left here and park near the end of the one-way system, leaving a five-minute walk into the centre. To visit **Caldas de Monchique★** (🏔🔺✕🖃🚻🚹WC **P**TM) by car, fork left at the next road (29.5km) and park by the roadside or in the centre car park (30km). Caldas underwent a major renovation some years ago, to restore the village to the spa centre it once was.

Leave Caldas by the one-way system and turn left to continue to wind up in the direction of Monchique, again passing the fork down left to Caldas (31km) a few moments later. A further 1.3km brings you to a superb viewpoint over Caldas on the left, the **Miradouro das Caldas** (✕🚻🖃).

At **Nave** (34.5km) there is a left turn to Marmelete opposite a quarry on the right, but keep ahead for Monchique. Just after a petrol station on the left, as you enter Monchique, come to a crossroads (36.5km).* Keep straight on up to the Largo 5 de Outubro in **Monchique★** (🚶🔺✕🖃⊕🚻WC; Walks 7-9). Park in the underground car park up the Fóia road, by the tourist office on the left, or further along by the Lisbon road on the right. It is

*A right turn here would take you to Alferce (🚻; 16km return) or 28.4km down to meet the N266 above Porto de Lagos; see touring map). There are wonderful views along this route.

Spectacular beach between Praia da Marinha and Praia da Albandeira

worthwhile trying the first part of Walk 7 as far as the convent. This guides you up through old Monchique to a good vantage point from where it's possible to enjoy views (📷) across the valley in the direction of Picota (Walk 9).

Continue through the square and up left towards Fóia (38km). Go right at the round-about soon encountered. The road now rises rapidly above Monchique. Fantastic views open out to the left (📷) as you climb through eucalyptus. When you reach the point where the vegetation starts to become more sparse (44km), there is a *fonte* and *miradouro* on the left; Walk 7 begins on the next track off left, reached almost immediately.

The final 2km drive up to the summit, through mainly low-lying heather and cistus, provides almost uninterrupted views (📷) over the countryside to the left. On the approach to **Fóia** (✗📷🍽), keep left to the car park. The summit is unfortunately home to a forest of television and radio masts, as well as a souvenir complex. But if you follow the notes for Short walk 8-2 (page 72) for about ten minutes, these will take you off the summit and to the fine views shown on page 73).

PERA MARSH NATURE RESERVE —
Bird-watching and a walk

To reach the reserve, turn seawards at the roundabout on the N125 towards Armação de Pera. At the second roundabout, turn left towards Albufeira and at the second roundabout along this road turn right towards Praia Grande (signposted). Continue along the narrow road and, on a right-hand bend in the direction of Armação de Pera, stay ahead on a track towards the coast — to a large parking area with information board, boardwalk and steps over the sand dunes to the beach.

Return to the main N266 (54km) by going right at the roundabout, then turn right in the direction of Portimão, following your outward route back to **Lagôa** (91km). An optional return is via Alferce (see footnote opposite), down to Odelouca (on the N124) and back via Silves to Lagôa.

21

Car tour 3: VILLAGES OF THE BARROCAL

Faro • Estói • Amendoeira • (Fonte de Benémola) • Salir • Alte • Paderne • Boliqueime • Faro

105km/65mi; about 2 hours 20 minutes' driving: leave Faro from the harbour (see town plan on the reverse of the touring map).

Walks en route: 13-15, 19-21; Walk 18 is nearby

Picnic suggestions: Fonte Grande (*P*14), Paderne Castle (*P*15), Rocha da Pena (*P*19), Salir (*P*20), Fonte de Benémola (*P*TM), Barreiras Brancas (*P*TM)

On the whole, the country roads used on this tour are well surfaced. Petrol is usually available inland, but make sure you have enough before setting out, especially on Sundays and holidays.

Opening hours
Milreu: open 09.30-12.30, 14.00-18.00; closed Mondays and holidays

A pink palace, some Roman ruins, a Moorish castle, gently-rolling pastoral countryside, and sleepy inland villages weave a fascinating tapestry into the central limestone region of Algarve — the Barrocal, described on pages 88 and 89.

The tour starts from **Faro**. If a visit to old Faro is part of your tour, the best place to park is in Largo de São Francisco; otherwise, avoid the centre of Faro with its confusing one-way system. A proliferaton of new road systems around Faro should make navigation quite easy. Start the tour by joining the N2 to São Brás, which also gives access to the A22 at Junction 14.

The N2 leads you quickly out across the plain to the Algarvian foothills and to the right turn to São Brás and Estói. Fork off right to Estói after 10km and turn right at the crossroads shortly afterwards. At the ruins of **Milreu** (10.2km 🚻), park outside on the left. (See Walk 21, page 114, for more details about this interesting site with many excavated remains to be seen.) On leaving Milreu continue into **Estói★** (11km ◼️🍴WC). Entering the main square, you can see the gates of the palace up to your left. Turn right and park further along this road. The gates give access to the gardens, where the photograph opposite was taken. They are worth a visit for their curiosity value, but the lower gardens may be closed for restoration. The palace itself has been converted into a luxury *pousada*, where the public are welcome to have a meal, drink or snack.

Return by the same route back to the main road to São Brás, and turn right immediately after crossing the bridge at the minor crossroads. You pass a petrol station on the left, just before meeting the main N2, where you turn right. Just 100m further on (after passing under the A22), take the left turn signposted to Bordeira (12.5km). A scenic route along winding country roads, through lovely rural countryside like that shown on pages 116-117, raises you gently into the rolling hills (📷). Just after a sharp bend to the left, meet significant-looking crossroads (19km) and keep ahead to the main Loulé/São Brás road (N270; 20km). Turn left, and be ready to turn right almost immediately (signposted 'São Romão' and 'Alportel'), back onto a country road. Rise up through **São Romão**

Tiled fountain in Estói Palace gardens

FONTE DE BENÉMOLA — *Circular walk for motorists* (● 4.4km; 50min-1h30min)

Buried deep in the countryside is a little known beauty spot by a river, the Fonte de Benémola. It is just a short red/yellow waymarked walk, ideal as a break during Car tour 3 or a short walk or for a picnic outing. An excellent **map and gps track** can be downloaded free from the WIP website (see the panel on page 39): download 'Lou PR16'.

Follow the notes for Car tour 3 to the 32km-point, on the N524, where you keep ahead towards Tor, instead of turning right. Look for a track on the right about 1km further on, signposted 'Fonte de Benémola'. Park off the road, by the abandoned house on the left, as you enter the track — or at a convenient place on the road.

Start walking down the track along the side of a shallow valley (the locals drive here, but we would like to discourage you from doing so). The deep green foliage of the orange trees and the ordered cultivation down on the left contrasts sharply with the scrubland up to the right. It is this scrubland, however, which shelters a wealth of wild flowers, including *Astragalus lusita-*

---

and come to a fork (21km), where you go left towards Amendoeira. Striking deeper into the hinterland, the rural aspect gives way to a more barren landscape. *Matos,* interspersed with pockets of cultivation, becomes more predominant as you near **Amendoeira** (24km). Reach the main Loulé/Barranco do Velho road and turn right (N396; 27km). Stay on this road for a short while, through **Porto Nobre** (28km), where pine trees lining the road give a more alpine feel to the surroundings. Fork off left towards 'Querença' and 'Tor' after 30km, and ignore a left turn to Querença shortly afterwards.

Keep along the road towards Tor, until you turn right towards 'Alte' and 'Lisbon' in 32km. (Keep ahead here for a further 1km, if you wish to visit the Fonte de Benémola, a lovely picnic setting (*P*TM); see circular walk suggestion above.) Here is yet another twisting road which wends its way through undulating countryside, past almond groves and through hamlets (☎). Watch out for some sharp bends along this stretch. The route of Walk 20 joins in from the left after 37km and stays with the road for 400m before departing off left on a field track. On arriving at the main N124, the São Bartolomeu de Messines/Barranco do Velho road (38km), turn left.

First head for Salir and pass the point where Walk 20 again meets the main road from the left (38.5km) and continues on the track opposite. The white water tower of Salir is easily distinguishable ahead, as you drive along past a scattering of white traditional houses. At the roundabout

nicus, with its creamy-yellow pea-like flowers, the cheerful yellow *Anemone palmata*, and a number of orchids. At a fork (**10min**), keep left. Head down towards a stream and the leafy shade of a natural beauty spot, where you cross a bridge over the stream. Turn left when the track divides beyond the bridge. Orange, lemon and carob trees cluster together on the left, the scent of the citrus flowers providing an added delight in spring. Keep left at the next division, staying ahead, with the river on your left, to reach the *fonte* and then the picnic area beyond it (*P3*). It is possible to explore further upstream, where the river flows through a small ravine and where there are some caves close by to the right.

To continue, cross the river on the good stepping stones *opposite the picnic area* and go left again on the track, downstream. Keep the river on your left and stay on the main track. A basket-maker can usually be found sitting outside his hut just below the return track, where baskets of varying sizes can be bought at reasonable prices. When you emerge by a bridge on the N524, turn left to cross the bridge, and follow the road round to the left, back to where you parked (five minutes away).

---

at 42km go left up to **Salir** (♦✕☎☐); note that this turn is signposted to Loulé and comes up when you have almost passed the village. This road leads uphill and skirts round the village, which is on the left. Follow the road and keep right towards Loulé. Park on the roadside below the village, about 0.9km from the main road. Head left up into the village on foot to explore the centre (photograph page 113) and perhaps take in the castle (*P20*). If you are doing Walk 20, park further along the wide road, about 1.3km from the main road (where the road bends right, down to 'Ponte de Salir' and 'Loulé'). For more details about Salir, see the notes for Walk 20 on page 110.

Return to the main N124 by the same route to continue, and turn left. As you drive along (☎), you can't fail to notice the huge ridge of Rocha da Pena (Walk 19) to the right. About 1km beyond Salir, at **Taipa**, note the access road on the right to Rocha, where Walk 19 begins at a *fonte* (*P19*).

Then come into **Pena**, where there is a local craft and information centre located in the old school (the last building on the right at the far end of the village). **Benafim** is soon reached (51km ☎), and here the road narrows to pass between the houses. At 56km, note the narrow road off left — just before a sharp right-hand bend in the road, which can catch you unawares: it is our return route on this tour.

Some 200m further along, on entering the confines of Alte, there is a road off right direct to Fonte Grande. The

BARREIRAS BRANCAS — *Circular walk for motorists (● 4km; 50min-1h30min)*

This is a very short walk for those driving around the Loulé area. To get there, turn north at the central roundabout in Loulé (note the kilometre reading), to pass the bus station on the left. Then, at the crossroads before the monument, turn right for 'Querença'. This sets you on the Barranco do Velho road. Once beyond an avenue of cypress trees, look for a parking spot just before the start of a similar avenue (3km out of Loulé). Park on the right, near a small engineering works and restaurant, opposite a café. A windmill on a hill is your destination.

Start the walk from the engineering works, by heading down the right-hand track between the workshop on the left and the restaurant on the right. The track leads between orange groves to a bridge over a stream which is crossed in 3min. Continue ahead, and ignore two tracks on the right as you start to ascend. Turn right on a road

waymarked with a yellow stripe (opposite a very modern villa; 8min). Keep an eye out on the left for a narrower walled-in path within two minutes; it leads you up the hillside in a gentle ascent. This old route hides some interesting flowers like the broad leaved *Epipactis helleborine* and the bright yellow *Anemone palmata*. Stay right in 11min, when the walled-in path runs into track and, as you continue to rise, you can enjoy views of Loulé to the right and the sea beyond. Meet a surfaced road in 14min, turn left in the direction of the windmill and, less than a minute later, stay ahead to a rough track (where the road swings right). At the next fork go left, above the peach-coloured house. In 16min, when the track divides, turn right; stay alongside the rock wall on the left to its end, then follow the path off left up to the windmill (19min; TM). Whilst nothing much remains to see of

the mill workings, there is a splendid panorama to be enjoyed from this location (see below). It is a good site for orchids, too, including the man orchid, *Aceras anthropophorum*, and the sombre bee orchid, *Ophrys fusca*.

Leave from the door of the mill and follow the path which heads in the direction of Loulé. The path leads down and round to the right, to pass beneath the windmill, now up on the right. Keep ahead as the path runs into surfaced road. Follow the road downhill, briefly meeting the upward route, to a T-junction (11min below the mill). Turn right, still on surfaced road, and enjoy the rural surrounds. Cross a wide field track, to continue ahead along another track. Some five minutes later, note the second of two walled-in paths leaving from the right: this is the path you took up to the mill. Turn left soon, to follow the outward route back to the car.

main tour goes first into Alte and then on to Fonte Grande but, if you wish to go there straight away, turn right here, follow the road round and cross the bridge. This brings you to the first large fountain and small picnic area on the right. A much larger picnic area and fountain (P14), with better facilities, is to the right, past and above the first fountain (photographs pages 92-95, map page 94).

First explore Alte itself, by continuing another 0.7km along the main road, past the Fonte Grande turn-off. The road runs below the village, which rises up to the right, and crosses a bridge where there is an old mill and some waterfalls. Turn right at the roundabout; this leads directly into the centre of Alte and the start of Walk 14. In just 200m, pass the left turn up to Santa Margarida (◉ and Walk 13; photograph page 89) as you enter **Alte**★ (✝♠✕ ⛺◉▣). Park where possible before the Santa Margarida turn-off or near the market stalls, where the road is wide. The village centre lies ahead, with its cafés and maze of narrow streets. It is possible to drive through the village to Fonte Grande, or you can walk there in under 15 minutes.

When you are ready to leave Alte, return to the roundabout on the N124 and turn left. Retrace your route to the 56km point, just after a sharp left bend, and turn right into a surfaced road (60km). This road wends its way across the shallow valley south of Alte, through low-lying vegetation, which allows for good views (◉) over the countryside. At the fork reached after 61.5km keep round to the right.

Care is needed in the centre of the village of **Monte Brito**, where there is a right-angled bend and no view round the corner. As you drive along a straight stretch of road, it is easy to feel that you are on the major road but beware: in just over 65km a road joins from the right, and there is a 'Stop' sign for you to obey — with no road markings. The sign is often obscured by foliage. Keep ahead, then turn right about 1km further on. There is a further right and left turn as the route heads across country to Paderne in the distance.

As you reach **Paderne**★ (69km ✝⊕▣), keep to the road which skirts round to the right. On meeting the main road in Paderne, turn right downhill to meet the Boliqueime road. Park near the stadium opposite this junction, to explore Paderne or stretch your legs with one of the many versions of Walk 15 (P15; photograph page 97, maps pages 97 and 99). To drive to Paderne Castle, turn right past the cemetery on the left. A little further on there is a road off left to the 'Fonte' and Paderne Castle.

To return to Faro, turn left opposite the stadium towards Boliqueime, passing Paderne up to the left. (But those returning to Albufeira and environs should continue west to the main N270 at Purgatório, 0.5km further on, and turn left.) Reach **Boliqueime** and turn left onto the N125 (79km) in the direction of Faro. Alternatively, go left to Junction 11 on the A22, for a faster return to Faro. Leave at Junction 13 to return to **Faro** (**105km**).

Albufeira

Faro • Olhão • (Tavira) • Vila Real de Santo António • Castro Marim • Cachopo • Barranco do Velho • São Brás de Alportel • Faro

175km/109mi; about 3 hours 30 minutes' driving: leave Faro from the harbour (see town plan on the reverse of the touring map).

Walks en route: 20-24

Picnic suggestions: ruined watermill near Tareja (*P*22)

Once off the N125, the inland roads become more winding and twisting. Make sure you have enough petrol before heading inland to Cachopo.

Vila Real is a bustling riverside town only a short ferry ride from Spain; nearby we find the tranquillity of a backwater, where the remains of a 14th-century castle stand sentinel to its past glory and importance. This tour penetrates deep into countryside still untouched by tourism, where you can relish an astoundingly beautiful landscape.

Start out from **Faro** along the N125 towards 'Espanha' (Spain), which will take you all the way to Vila Real and the Spanish border.

Olhão (♦🏐🏔🔺✕△🚩⊕M🏊WC) is reached in 8km. Keep ahead on the main road at the first roundabout but, if you want to explore Olhão, turn right here to reach the centre. (A left turn at the same point would take you out to Estói, setting for Walk 21.) Pass a left turn to Moncarapacho and São Brás and then a right turn to Porto de Olhão (9km). Porto de Olhão is where you catch a ferry out to the Barrier Islands, where there are sandy beaches and shallow waters ideal for bathing — see page 34. Beyond Olhão the road surface becomes very good until you reach **Luz de Tavira** (22km), where you need to take care, as the road narrows. Note the Manueline doorway of the church on the left here. Continue along through flat cultivated countryside and scattered hamlets, where oranges, almonds and vines are important crops.

At the first roundabout, go right if you wish to visit Tavira★ (♦🏛🏐🏔✕🚩⊕🏊WC)*. The main tour keeps ahead here, to reach the motorway roundabout (29km) and then a high-level road bridge. Note the left turn to Cachopo immediately after crossing the bridge; this is the road you will take on the return route. After the next roundabout (30km) the road off right is the exit from Tavira. Soon you are passing the large Ozadi Hotel on the

*Park near the new market hall then continue over the new bridge to rejoin the N125 and continue the tour. Add about 3km to the overall distance for the tour, if you visit the town.

left (32km), a landmark for those wishing to visit the Tavira National Forest for Walk 23. The left turn to the forest is 350m after the road into the hotel: a brown sign indicates 'Mata da Conceição'.

After some 40km, the road narrows and curves to cross a bridge, then speedily carries you on in the direction of Vila Real. Just after the motorway slip road and a water sports centre on the left (46km), there is a left turn to 'Castro Marim' and 'Beja' (our return route). Keep ahead on the main road, to come into **Vila Real de Santo António★** (✝⛰▲✕⛽⊕M☕WC), at 52km passing a roundabout with a left turn to Castro Marim. The road system in Vila Real is set out in a grid, so direction-finding is fairly straightforward. Follow the sign to the 'centro'; it directs you right, past the hospital on the left, and then left, down to the river. Entering on foot, you can follow the pedestrian walkway to the centre of town, by keeping ahead where the traffic is diverted to the right. Parking is allowed in some streets and along the riverside road. We find it easier to park on the outskirts and walk — especially if the town is busy. If you wish to visit Spain, a ferry still crosses the river regularly, taking about 15 minutes to cross, despite a road bridge further up the river.

Return to the Castro Marim roundabout (the 52km-point), and turn right on the N122. Gum and palm trees line the elevated road running straight through the nature reserve.* Castro Marim itself can be seen ahead. The start of Walk 24 is on the left, 1.6km from the roundabout on the N125. Turn left into **Castro Marim★** (57km ✝■☕ WC), and park in the car park. The castle entrance is up to the right. There are photographs of the area on pages 127 and 130. Castro Marim is one of the best areas for bird-watching in Algarve; see notes for Walk 24 on page 127.

Leave Castro Marim along the N125-6 in the direction of Tavira. At the point where a fork goes off right to 'Rio Seco' (59km), keep round to the left. Go over a level crossing (62km) and meet the N125 after 64km, where you turn right in the direction of Faro. Keep on the N125

*A Reserve Centre (*i*) has opened on the banks of the Guadiana River. To get there, continue north on the N122, going under the motorway. Take the first turning right (signposted 'Reserva Natural'), then turn right again, back under the motorway. The centre is the huge brown building down the track/road to the left. The Castro Marim Reserve, around the Reserve Centre, is a good location for bird watching. There is a board outside the centre showing short walks, and leaflets are available inside. The centre closes from 12.30 to 14.00.

as far as the high level bridge at Tavira (about 3km after the Ozadi Hotel on the right), and turn right on the N397 towards Cachopo (81km). Keep right at the 'Picota' sign. The road initially crosses a plain, with the river on the left, heading towards the hills.

Eucalyptus trees line the road as it starts to climb, passing the occasional vineyard and olive grove. Uniformly-rounded hills roll into the distance as you penetrate this unknown but extremely photogenic area of Algarve (📷). A delightful and unusual mosaic, created by varying shades of vegetative cover, cloaks the landscape (📷), adding a delicious hint of unreality and adventure. After 111km, you start to descend, to pass a café and cross the Ribeira de Odeleite. The changing scene is coloured by clusters of pink heather, *Erica australis,* as you pass a fountain on the right (115km). Just when you begin to feel really isolated and in the middle of nowhere, terraced hillsides, cleared of *matos,* announce the proximity of

Unknown Algarve: these gloriously green rolling hills lie between Tavira and Cachopo.

habitation. **Cachopo** (121km ⛨✖️⛟) is reached just after you pass an impressive cemetery on the right. Stretch your legs and explore this interesting backwater.

Leave Cachopo by turning left on the N124 towards Barranco do Velho; after 1km look out for a picturesque old stone bridge on the left. The road now winds along at a high level (📷) through the pleasant rural hamlets of **Catraia** and **Feiteira*** to Barranco do Velho. There is a windmill on the left (137km), before you start to descend into forest. When you reach **Barranco do Velho** (145km ⛰✖️⛟), the N124 goes off right towards Alte and São Bartolomeu de Messines, but keep round left on the N2, to plunge down into the forest towards São Brás and Faro.

On reaching **São Brás de Alportel** (158km ⛨⛰🅿✖️⊕ ⛟wcP22; Walk 22), keep ahead for Faro. If you wish to stop in São Brás, turn left to 'Centro' and park there, or take the next left turn out of the square, into the main shopping street to park. See notes for Walk 22 on page 119 for more information about São Brás, and a large-scale map.

---

*Readers have recommended nine waymarked walks of varying lengths near Cachopo: three of these are based on Feiteira, three on Casas Baixas and three on Mealha. They say all are signposted and clearly waymarked.

Orange groves on the drive up to Monte São Miguel. Left: cork oak

MONTE SÃO MIGUEL

Standing alone on the eastern side of Faro, this mound is a landmark which can be seen for miles around. It would be easy to identify even without the TV transmitter perched on the summit. It's not its height (only 410m/1345ft), but the fact that it stands on the edge of a large area of plain, that makes it so visible. Conversely, it is a good viewpoint, the best in the east. It doesn't offer anything in the way of walking possibilities, but it is worth the drive up to enjoy the views, if you are in the region.

Perhaps you could combine this excursion with a visit to the Sunday market at Moncarapacho (see 'Country fairs and markets' on page 13). Moncarapacho lies 7km north of the N125 (to the northwest of Olhão).

Start out for São Miguel from Moncarapacho by heading north towards Santa Catarina. After about 1km, fork left into a narrow surfaced road (where there is a hard-to-read signpost for São Miguel). This road leads over the motorway all the way up to the summit after 5km, but be sure to keep left at the fork near the top. Apart from good views, there are some interesting wild flowers to be seen, if you make short forays into the *matos*.

33

RAINY DAY SHOPPING OPTIONS

Algarve has moved rapidly into the world of big commercial centres.

Forum Algarve (Jumbo), on the airport side of Faro, Algarve Shopping at Guia, near Albufeira, and Portimão are all popular venues. These are reached from the N125 and house cinema complexes, restaurants and cafés, besides a huge supermarket and up-market shops.

From São Brás, swiftly descend onto the plain, first passing the point where Walk 21 crosses the road on its return (162km), and then passing the left turn to Estói. Walk 21 crosses the road here (165km), on its outward route. You regain **Faro** after 175km.

THE BARRIER ISLANDS

There is a group of islands and sand banks lying offshore in the general area south and east of Faro and, if you fly into Faro airport, you will have an excellent overall view of them as you start to descend. The whole of this area is a nature reserve called 'Parque Natural da Ria Formosa'. The outermost islands are known as the 'barrier islands', since they protect the inland side from the worst of the rough seas, particularly when the Atlantic breakers are in full swell.

Two of the islands in the central area are popular for bathing. Both are reached by regular ferry from Olhão. The nearest, Ilha de Armona, is reached in about 15 minutes by ferry, and it is almost pure sand. The beach on the sheltered side runs into shallow, warm waters; it is an ideal family beach. The seaward side offers the longer beach, stretching almost all the way to Tavira. This means that you can almost always find a quiet spot of your own.

The second island, Ilha da Culatra, is reached after a 45-minute ferry ride and has permanent habitation. Although just as beautiful, this island is generally less visited because of the longer ferry journey. Full details of the boat timetables are available from the tourist office in Olhão and from the ticket kiosk on the harbour.

Ilha de Armona is also accessible from Tavira. Frequent buses run from the square, Praça da Republica, and travel along the coast to connect up with the ferry, which runs constantly throughout the day in the season. This eastern end of the island has more facilities and is perhaps a little more crowded. Again, the inland side is well sheltered, and the seaward side enjoys the full force of the Atlantic.

The most easterly of these barrier islands, Cabanas, can be reached from the town of Cabanas just to the east of Tavira.

34

Faro • Santana da Serra • Almodôvar • Mértola • Castro Marim • Faro

287km/178mi; about 5h driving

Walk en route: 24

The outward drive uses the fast route into Alentejo via the A22 motorway across Algarve and then the A2 (toll) Lisbon motorway, but later cuts across the very different Alentejana countryside to reach Mértola. There are one or two recommended stops mentioned in the text. The southerly return route follows the line of the Guadiana through pastoral countryside back to the eastern side of Algarve. Alternatively use the slower IC1 road north (see footnote).

Continuously occupied for more than 2000 years, layers of history are rarely so transparent as at Mértola on the banks of the Guadiana River. This historic walled town has a Roman port in a remarkable state of preservation, a castle, a mosque converted into a church and several fine museums (free entry). Located in Alentejo close to the border with Algarve, Mértola is a little-visited town in spite of its powerful attractions. The authors' guide is strongly recommended to get the most out of this visit (see 'Background reading' on page 6). There are good restaurants in the town, and it is worth considering an overnight stop to explore the region's other places of interest.

Leave Faro by heading north, to pick up the A22 motorway at Junction 13 or 14, where you turn left. When you reach the intersection with the northbound A2 at Junction 10/15 (45km), follow signs for Lisbon.* Then motor steadily north, to exit at Junction 13, signposted to Almodôvar. Turn left at the roundabout for Mértola. **Gomes Aires** (108km ⚑) lies just to the right. Beyond this village you have a taste of typical Alentejana landscape — rolling tracts of land dotted with umberella-shaped oak trees, providing summer shade for the pigs. (There is an excellent folk museum at Santa Clara-a-Nova: to get there, take a short detour off to the right. The museum is often locked but will be opened on demand — just ask.)

Almodôvar (118.5km ✝✗🚻🅿M) is larger than expected, but the N267 to Mértola is well signposted —

---

*To avoid the motorway, stay on the A22 to Junction 9, then take the IC1 (old IP1) north. This slower route is about the same distance. Keep alert on approaching Santana da Serra (93.5km), note the junction with a turning left to Santa Clara and, just 1km further on the IC1, at the top of the hill, turn right into a narrow surfaced road signposted to Almodôvar. Just 0.6km further on, turn right again on the N393. Gomes Aires is soon reached, where you join the A2 (toll) motorway route of the main tour. Follow the main tour from the 108km-point to continue.

even though the route weaves through the town. More open countryside follows, but at 138km there is a chance for another short diversion on the right — into São Miguel do Pinheiro, to see a restored, working windmill busy producing flour. Bread is baked here in faithfully-restored ovens and sold in the shop. There is a coffee shop and restaurant close by.

The atmospheric old walls of **Mértola** (160km 🏛️⛪ ✕🅿️🚌M) only appear once you are close to the town. There is a car park on the left, from where it's just a short walk up to the right into the compact centre. The tourist office is a good first stop, to see if the museums are open (some just open on demand out of the main season). Apart from the highlights mentioned in the panel opposite, the Roman museum is worth a visit. It occupies the excavated remains of a Roman villa beneath the town hall. (There

Mértola

are no signs of it until you enter the main town hall door, from where you walk down to the lower level.)

Leave by the same road and fork left on the N122 after 2.5km, following signs to Vila Real. More engaging open countryside fills the windscreen, with just one or two small villages to add variety. Pick up the IC27 from Santa Marta, and you soon reach the **Alcoutim/Cachopo junction** (188km), where you have a choice of routes. The main tour continues straight ahead on the IC27 to **Castro Marim** (Walk 24) and **Vila Real**, where you join the A22 motorway (228.5km). Head back west to Junction 14 and **Faro** (287km).

But the run alongside the Guadiana River and the Spanish border, via Alcoutim (where the long-distance Algarve Way walking route begins), is very scenic and recommended if time allows. It is a little slower and adds around 8km to the tour.

A third route, back to central Algarve via Cachopo and Barranco do Velho (see Car tour 4), is also scenic, but very slow going.

OCCUPYING A DOMINANT POSITION on the once-navigable Guadiana River, Mértola enjoyed a long period of prosperity from Roman times right through into the 13th century. Under Islamic rule, Mértola was twice capital of a kingdom which included Beja. Echoes of the past are inescapable; every street, every corner has a story to tell.

The best place to start is the castle which crowns the hill. On the way up it is often possible to look inside the church where the *mirhab* is still visible behind the altar. Note the Moorish arch of the side door.

Within the castle grounds there are ongoing excavations, where a huge cryptoporticum has been slowly and painfully excavated. Enquire at the tourist office about guided tours which are run twice-daily when there is demand.

The Roman museum is exceptionally well presented within the excavated remains of a Roman villa beneath the town hall. Showcases set amongst the ruins themselves display some of the finds. The Museum of Islamic Art has the finest display of Islamic pottery in Portugal. No doubt the storks' nests will still be resident on the clock tower nearby, and there are good views down over the Roman port at this point.

Just 17km east of Mértola lies the Mina de São Domingos. Once worked by the Romans, this huge copper and sulphur mine was run by a British company for over a hundred years before it closed in 1965. A narrow-gauge railway transported the copper and sulphur south to Pomarão, from where it was shipped down-river to Vila Real. The mine is now a museum with an on-site hotel.

✿ Walking

Algarve is justly famous for its fine beaches and beautiful coastline. It is not normally thought of in terms of open countryside, pretty villages and ideal rambling opportunities. Many visitors will be surprised by the fine and varied landscapes to be enjoyed across the length of the region. To the north and east, the rolling, interlocking *matos*-covered hills catch the long rays of the sun, to present an ever-changing interplay of light and shade. The limestone of the central Barrocal plays host to most of the charming villages — and to the best of the wild flowers. Further west, the granite mountains of the Serra de Monchique provide the ruggedness and grandeur. Further west still, the landscape takes on a windswept appearance, which is at its most extreme as you approach Sagres. It is impossible to ignore the fine coastline, and we have made the most of those parts which are still unspoilt, so that you can enjoy some of the scenery which has contributed to the fame of this beautiful region.

There are enough walks in this book to keep you going for a month or more. The groundwork has been done, so from day one you can be out in the countryside, enjoying your holiday to the full. But please accept some words of caution. Follow the walks as described or by using paths or tracks shown on the maps; never try to get from one walk to another across uncharted terrain — even though it may look possible. Promising-looking tracks or paths may only lead to someone's smallholding, and distances can be very deceptive in the high hills and across coastal gullies.

Locals no longer use many of the routes, sections of which are in danger of becoming overgrown. We spend time chopping back foliage when we are in Algarve and would be grateful if other wielders of secateurs made the odd snip here and there to help keep routes open for everyone. Thank you to those of you who already do!

There are walks in this book for everyone.

Beginners: Start on the walks graded ● or ●, and check all the short and alternative walks.

Experienced walkers: If a walk is very long, do be sure of your fitness before you attempt it. Don't attempt the more strenuous walks in high summer; do protect yourself from the sun, and always carry an ample supply of water and plenty of fruit. Please remember too that storm damage could make any walk described in this book unsafe, so be sure to err on the side of safety. If you have not reached one of our landmarks after a reasonable time, then you must return to the last 'sure' point and start again.

Experts: The walks around Monchique offer the best challenge and, if you are out to test your stamina, it is possible to join walks together to make a longer day.

Grading, waymarking, maps, GPS

We've tried to give you a quick overview of each walk's **grade** in the Contents. But many of our walks are long, so we've split them up into several shorter and alternative versions. In the Contents we've only had space to show the *lowest* grade of a main or multiple-section walk: for full details, see the walk itself. Here is a brief overview of the four gradings:

● very easy — more or less level (perhaps with a short climb to a viewpoint); good surfaces underfoot; easily followed

● easy-moderate — ascents/descents of no more than about 300-500m/ 1000-1800ft; good surfaces underfoot; easily followed

● moderate-strenuous — ascents/descents may be over 500m/1800ft; variable surfaces underfoot — you must be sure-footed and agile; possible route-finding problems in poor visibility

● expert — only suitable for very experienced hillwalkers with a head for heights; hazards may include landslides or very narrow paths with no respite from constant exposure (there are *no* black bullets in this guide)

Any of the above grades may, if applicable, be followed by:

❖ *possibility* of vertigo — for those with no head for heights at all

❖❖ *danger* of vertigo — you must have a very good head for heights

In recent years, Portugal has had EU support for repairing, **signposting** and **waymarking** several walking routes with standard European red and yellow flashes (two horizontal stripes mean *continue this way*; right- or left-angled stripes indicate a *change of direction*; X means *do not go this way*).

Algarve Way (GR13) ... *and many more walking ideas*

The Algarve Way long-distance footpath runs for some 300km between the Spanish border and Cape St Vincent and uses standard European waymarking (red/white or red/yellow flashes). At viaalgarviana.org you can download free notes (in English), maps, and gpx files. **Do not expect to see waymarking on the ground**: it is confined to critical turnings, and there are long stretches with no waymarks. In the current economic climate, volunteers to clean and waymark are thin on the ground. The same website has many links to other long-distance and day walks, with enough information to whet your appetite. But a simply superb site is www.wiportugal.org (with English pages). Here you will find **free gpx and map downloads** for (as of press date) no fewer than 55 day walks and several long-distance hikes passing through Algarve and in other parts of Portugal.

Our text and maps include these waymarked routes (all prefaced with 'GR' or 'PR') *where they existed at press date*.

The **maps** in this book are based on Openstreetmap mapping (see page 2), but have been very heavily annotated from our notes and GPS work in the field. We hope that these maps, which we have found to be *very* accurate on the ground, will be a boon to walkers. It is a pity that we have to reproduce them at only 1:50,000 to keep the book to a manageable size; quite a few walkers buy both the paperback *and* download our pdf files so that they can print out the maps at a larger size.

Free **GPS track** downloads and **height profiles** are available for all our walks: see the Algarve page on the Sunflower website. Please bear in mind, however, that GPS readings should *never* be relied upon as your sole reference point — especially as some of our walks go more or less cross-country on no particular path. Conditions can also change at any time. GPS is hardly needed in Algarve anyway, but what *is* great fun is dragging our GPX files over Google Earth to preview the walks in advance!

What to take

If you are already in Portugal when you find this book, and you haven't any special equipment such as a rucksack and walking boots, you can still do some of the walks — but better still, buy some of the equipment you need locally. Boots, shoes, and trainers can all be bought fairly cheaply, provided you do not require a large size. Continental size 45 is often the upper limit for men and 41 for women. Don't attempt any of the difficult walks without the proper gear or with brand-new footwear. Always check the *grade of the walk:* if it is easy and follows fairly level tracks or footpaths, you should be able to wear trainers. (Do *not* wear sandals, as explained under 'Things that bite or sting' below.) If we mention loose-stone paths or steep descents, then walking boots are absolutely essential; you will need to rely on the grip and ankle support they provide. All other walks should be made with stout shoes, preferably with thick rubber soles to grip on wet and slippery surfaces. You may find the following check list useful:

walking boots (which must be broken-in) and spare boot laces
waterproof rain gear (outside summer months)

swimming costume
bandages and band aids
plastic plates, cups, etc
knives and openers

long-sleeved shirt
  (for sun protection)
long trousers, tight at the ankles
  (sun and tick protection)
plastic groundsheet
antiseptic cream
woollen hat and gloves
water bottle with water
  purifying tablets
'Dog Dazer' (see page 43)
secateurs (see page 38)

anorak (zip opening)
sunhat, sunglasses, suncrean
universal sink plug
insect repellent
binoculars
fleece
extra pair (long) socks
compass, whistle, torch
small rucksack
compact folding umbrella
mobile/smart phone, GPS

Please bear in mind that we have not done *every* walk in the book under *all* conditions. We might not realise just how hot or exposed some walks might be in high summer or how cold in winter. For this reason we have listed above all the gear you *might* need, depending on the season, and we rely on your good judgement to modify the list accordingly.

Beware of the sun and the effects of dehydration. Don't be deceived by light cloud cover; you can still get sunburnt. While it's tempting to wear shorts for walking, always carry long trousers and a long-sleeved shirt and put them on when you have had enough sun — and *always* wear a sunhat. Don't forget that, with the sun behind you, the backs of your legs and your neck are getting badly sunburnt. (Pushing through prickly holly oak in shorts isn't much fun either.) Choose a shady spot for your lunch on hot days, and make sure that you carry with you a good supply of fruit and water.

Where to stay

There is a wide range of resorts to suit all tastes in Algarve, most of them situated along the coast. Those who prefer a more **rural atmosphere** will find a growing choice of accommodation inland, particularly in the area between **Silves** and **São Brás de Alportel** and around **Monchique**.

The **central part of the coastline** is also a good area in which to stay, because you can get to most parts of Algarve without too much travelling. **Albufeira** is the largest resort in this region, and has good bus connections, although it is not so convenient for trains. The nearest station is at Ferreira, 6km outside the resort. For a quieter place to stay, try some of the smaller places outside Albufeira like **Montechoro**. It makes a central base for walkers with a hire car and allows for easy escapes into the countryside.

Moving **westwards, Carvoeira** is a lively resort and **Alvor**, near **Portimão**, has grown apace. If you prefer small, quieter places, then look west of Lagos now, although this region is already being developed at an alarming rate. **Lagos** is a pleasing resort, which seems to combine spaciousness with the peace of somewhere much smaller. Once west of Lagos, the once-quiet resorts are developing rapidly. They are also further away from most of the walks, but the new motorway as far as Lagos has shortened travelling times.

Exploring the **eastern side of the region** is made easier from the central resorts by the motorway. **Faro** does have hotels and is a convenient centre for public transport, but does not have the traditional image of a resort. **Olhão**, to the east of Faro, is even less easy on the eye, but convenient for boats out to the beautiful beaches of the barrier islands. **Tavira**, possibly the most picturesque resort on the eastern side, is also a centre for boat trips out to the barrier islands. **Monte Gordo**, almost on the eastern border with Spain, is also a popular resort, but from here few of the walks are within easy reach.

Weather

The kindest months for walking in this part of Portugal are those either side of summer: March, April, May, September and October. However, walking through the mild winter months can be entirely delightful. There are likely to be many fine days, even in January, which are quite superb for walking. February, too, can provide many good opportunities and be the equal of any of the later spring months. By March the temperature is starting to rise, and it is certainly warm enough to air the shorts. Sunny days are plentiful, but there is still a chance of a day or two with rain, and these conditions prevail through April, even though the temperature is increasing steadily. May brings more warmth and sunshine, with only a small risk of unsettled weather. By June the weather is getting too hot for strenuous walks, but some of the coastal walks, where you will be cooled by the Atlantic sea breezes, can still be enjoyed — as they can throughout the summer months.

As the summer heat starts to decline in September, a new walking season opens up. This lasts through October and into November — until the start of the rainy season. The late autumn is often the wettest part of the year, but the average annual rainfall for the area, especially the coastal region, is very low, at 400-500mm (16-20 inches). *Be aware that after heavy rain, walks which cross rivers (16, 18, 19) may be impassable for a few days; Walk 24 will be sticky, slippery mud.*

Things that bite or sting

Dogs can be a nuisance. We were thankful to be carrying a 'Dog Dazer', which we found to be very effective, and it gave us considerable confidence. A Dog Dazer is a small, easily-portable electronic device which, at the press of a button, emits a noise which is inaudible to the human ear, but which startles aggressive dogs and persuades them to back off. Dog Dazers are available from several different sources on the web (where you can also read reviews). Otherwise, the best advice, if you feel threatened and have no walking stick, is to pick up a stone and pretend to throw it. More often than not, the dogs bark loudly but are rarely actually aggressive.

Snakes are something you will have to be on your guard against. We see very few in winter or spring, but we are advised that there are more around in summer. Most are probably harmless, but if there are any of the viper species around, then great care is needed. Most snakes are more frightened of you than you are of them, and they will move out of your way rapidly. But, if they don't, the best advice is to move quietly out of their way. The real danger comes should you accidentally step on a snake. For this reason, it is *imperative* that you do not walk in the countryside in open sandals, no matter how comfortable they might be for walking. Always have your feet and ankles well covered. It is also a sensible precaution to wear your long trousers tucked into your socks. Take special care near water, when you are about to sit down, or when you choose to rest your hand, so unthinkingly, on a dry-stone wall.

Scorpions are around, too, most likely seen in the height of summer, when they are usually seeking shade — so don't leave any of your clothing on the ground. Accidentally turning over rocks or stones may expose them but, generally, they offer no serious threat, since their sting is more painful than dangerous for most people.

In areas which are well forested, **ticks** can be a problem. As you brush through the woodlands, they can get onto your clothes. Again, if you follow our advice about wearing long trousers and a long-sleeved shirt, you should be able to keep them off your skin. If they do manage to get to your skin, then it is necessary to make them withdraw before you take them off. An easy way to do this is to touch them with a solvent such as methylated spirits or petrol.

Bees and **wasps** are around in summer, so make sure you carry the necessary creams and pills, especially if you are allergic to insect bites.

Hunting season

The hunting season lasts from October to the end of February, with shooting allowed on Sundays, Thursdays and Public Holidays. Walkers in the countryside should be aware of possible danger on these days. There are now many private and 'no hunting' zones which are usually indicated by the appropriate signs.

A country code for walkers and motorists

The experienced rambler is used to following a 'country code', but the tourist out for a lark may unwittingly cause damage, harm animals, and even endanger his own life. Do heed the following advice:

- **Do not light fires**; everything gets tinder-dry in summer. Stub out cigarettes with care.
- **Do not frighten animals**. The goats and sheep you may encounter on your walks are not tame. By making loud noises or trying to touch them or photograph them, you may cause them to run in fear and be hurt.
- **Walk quietly** through all farms, hamlets and villages, leaving all gates just as you found them. Gates do have a purpose, usually to keep animals in (or out of) an area. Remember, too, that a gate may be of a temporary nature — brushwood across the path — but it serves the same purpose, so please replace it after passing.
- **Protect all wild and cultivated plants**. Don't try to pick wild flowers or uproot saplings. They will die before you even get back to the hotel. When photographing wild flowers, watch where you put your feet so that you do not destroy others in the process. Obviously fruit and crops are someone's private property and should not be touched.
- **Never walk over cultivated land**.
- **Take all your litter away with you**.
- **Walkers — do not take risks**. Do not attempt walks beyond your capacity and **never** walk alone. *Always* tell a responsible person *exactly* where you are going and what time you plan to return. Remember, if you

become lost or injure yourself, it may be a long time before you are found. On any but a very short walk near villages, it's a good idea to carry a torch, whistle, GPS or compass, mobile, extra water and warm clothing — as well as some high-energy food like chocolate. Review the 'Important note to the reader' on page 2.

Portuguese for walkers

Despite the large numbers of tourists visiting Algarve, British tourists in particular, we found surprisingly little English spoken outside the major resorts. To ask directions in the countryside, you may well need to try your hand at Portuguese. A good technique is to memorise a few key questions, and then try to phrase your question so that it demands a 'yes' (*sim;* pronounced **seng**) or 'no' (*não;* pronounced **nowg**) answer. It is not always possible to conduct the whole conversation in this manner, so it pays to learn a few other answers that you might expect, or which you can use to form more questions to get yes/no answers. Examples of key questions and possible answers are given overleaf.

In Alte (Walk 14)

Key questions

English	Portuguese	approximate pronunciation
'Pardon me,	Faz o favor,	Fahz oh fah-**vohr**,
sir (madam).	senhor (senhora).	sehn-**yohr** (sehn-**yoh**-rah).
Where is	Onde é	**Ohn**-deh eh
the footpath to ...	a vereda para ...	ah veh-**ray**-dah **pah**-rah ...
(the road to ...	(a estrada para ...	(ah ish-**trah**-dah **pah**-rah
...		
the way to...	o caminho para ...	oh cah-**mee**-noh **pah**-rah
...		
the bus stop)?	a paragem)?	ah pah-**rah**-jeng?
Many thanks.'	Muito obrigado.	**Mween**-toh oh-bree-**gah**-doh
	(a woman says	
	muito obrigada).	(oh-bree-**gah**-dah).

Possible answers

English	Portuguese	approximate pronunciation
here	aqui	ah-**key**
there	ali	ah-**lee**
straight ahead	sempre em frente	sem-preh em **frenght**
behind	atrás	ah-**trahsh**
to the right	a dereita	ah deh-**ray**-tah
to the left	a esquerda	ah ish-**kehr**-dah
above	em cima	engh **see**-mah
below	em baixo	engh **bigh**-joh

Try to get a native speaker (possibly somebody at the hotel or a taxi driver) to help you learn the pronunciation. You must pronounce the name of your destination *very carefully*. For guidance with the pronunciation of place names in this book, see the Index.

When you have your mini-speech memorised, always ask the many questions that you can concoct from it in such a way that a yes/no answer will result. For example:

'Faz o favor, senhora. Onde é a estrada para Faro? É sempre em frente?' or 'Faz o favor, senhor. Onde é a verada para Alte? É em cima a esquerda?'

An inexpensive phrase book is a valuable aid from which you can choose other 'key' phrases and answers. And remember that it's always pleasant to greet people you may meet on your walks with a 'good morning' (bom dia/bohm **dee**-ah) or 'good afternoon' (boa tarde/boah **tard**).

Organisation of the walks

The walks in this book — more than 50 long and short routes — are spread across the whole of Algarve, with the greatest concentration around the central area. Begin by considering the large fold-out touring map inside the back cover. Here you can see the overall terrain, the road network, and the general location of all the walks.

Flipping through the pages, you will find that there is at least one photograph for each walk.

Having selected potential excursions from the map and photographs, look over the planning information at the beginning of each walk to find distance/walking time, grade (including a colour-coded bullet for quick reference), and how to get there and return. If the grade is beyond your scope, don't despair! There's almost always a short or alternative version of the walk and, in most cases, these are less demanding of ability and equipment. If it still looks too strenuous for you, look at the picnic suggestions which allow you to savour a walk's special landscape with the minimum of effort.

The text of the walk begins with an introduction to give you a flavour of the landscape and comments about special points of interest, before the route is described in detail. The text is illustrated with 1:50,000 maps (all with north at the top). These have been overprinted with the routes and key landmarks; see under 'Grading, waymarking, maps, GPS' on page 39.

Note that **we are fairly fit walkers** and that our time checks include only brief pauses, where you might stop to recover breath. They do *not* include photographic or picnic stops — or any stops of indeterminate length. **It is *not* intended that you match these frequent time-checks throughout the walk**; they are given to indicate the *time difference* from one point to another (and to facilitate reference to the short and alternative walks). This means that *you should allow up to twice as long as the stated time*. Don't forget to take bus connections at the end of the walk into account, particularly with regard to the last bus of the day. The most important factor is *consistency* of walking times, and we have checked our times at least twice. You'll soon see how your pace compares with ours and make adjustments for your stride … and the heat!

Below is a key to the **symbols** on the walking maps:

Symbol	Description	Symbol	Description
▅▅▅	main road	GR13	Algarve Way long-distance walk	○ ❷	start/end.waypoint
▭▭▭	secondary road			✗ ⼤	windmill.turbine
▦▦▦	major track	⛪ ⛪	church, monastery.chapel	🗼 Å	pylon.aerial
▬▬▬	jeep track			P	picnic spot (see page 8)
------	footpath	⊞ †	cemetery.cross		
2➤	route of main walk and direction	⛭	factory	📷	best views
2➤	alternative route	🚗🚗	bus stop.parking	📖	page reference: map continuation
2➤	other walk	🚂	railway station	❋�	mill.ancient site
		♪	well/spring *(fonte)*		

Walk 1: LUZ • *ATALAIA* • PORTO DE MÓS • PONTA DA PIEDADE • LAGOS

See also photographs on page 6 and the cover

Distance: 9.6km/6mi; just over 2h *(allow 3h or more)*

Grade: ● ‡ easy-moderate. The walk is mainly on footpaths, with some climbing involved, especially in the first part from Luz to the obelisk at 109m/358ft. Careful footwork required (some exposed path sections)

Equipment: See pages 41-42.

Picnic suggestion: obelisk (20min on foot; steep, short climb; *no shade*)

How to get there: 🚌 by bus from Lagos to Luz (Timetable 1). Journey time 15min. 🚗 by car: immediately on entering Luz follow the sign 'Praia da Luz' off left, down to a car park by the sea front (37° 5.240'N, 8° 43.548'W). If you do arrive by car, the chances are that you will have to walk back the same way: see Alternative walk 4 below.

Short walks: ● Both are easy, but *remember to allow plenty of time*.

1 Luz—*atalaia*—Luz (2.8km/1.75mi; 36min; a stiff climb). Follow the start of the walk to the obelisk and return the same way.

2 Luz — Porto de Mós — Luz (8.8km/5.5mi; 1h50min). ‡ Follow the main walk for 53min, and make this your turning point. There are café/bars where you can take refreshments before returning. The beach is stony close to the path, but sandy further out.

Alternative walks (all are ● ‡)

3 Luz — Ponta da Piedade — Luz (12.8km/8mi; 2h45min). Follow the walk to the lighthouse; return the same way. Easy-moderate.

4 Luz — Lagos — Luz (18.6km/11.5mi; 4h). If you go by car, you may have to walk back the same way, because of the limited bus services between Lagos and Luz (Timetable 1). Easy-moderate.

5 Porto de Mós — Ponta da Piedade — Porto de Mós (4km/2.5mi; 1h). An option for motorists. Park in the large car park at Porto de Mós (37° 5.172'N, 8° 41.338'W): on approaching Lagos from Portimão, immediately after crossing the bridge turn left at the roundabout and follow signs for Sagres. Negotiate the next three roundabouts by going right, left, right. Then keep ahead uphill to another roundabout, where Luz

Burgau

and Sagres are signposted to the right. Turn left here, and then turn right 1.4km further on, following the sign to Porto de Mós (2km). Walk from the car park to the lighthouse at Ponta da Piedade, following the main walk from the 53min-point; return the same way.

Longer walks (all ● ✦): The coastal footpath stretches all the way from Lagos to Salema. We have broken the route down into three stretches which are presented as Walks 1-3. All the sections have a totally different character with different points of interest and, if you want to spend a little time on the various beaches, exploring the villages or relaxing in the café/bars, then they are worth doing separately. But they can be joined together in various combinations — as follows. See map pages 60-61.

6   Salema to Luz via Burgau (10.1km/6.3mi; 2h40min). Taxi or bus to Salema (Timetable 2) and walk back to Luz using the map on pages 60-61 (Walk 3 and then Walk 2, both in reverse). Return from Luz by bus (Timetable 1). See (8) below for information about the Salema bus.

7   Burgau to Lagos via Luz (14km/8.7mi; 3h10min). Take a bus out to Burgau, as in Walk 3, and walk back to Lagos, using the map on pages 60-61 to walk to Luz (Walk 2 in reverse). Then pick up Walk 1.

8   Salema to Lagos (19.5km/12.1mi; 4h40min). Take a taxi or bus out to Salema (Timetable 2) and walk the whole distance back to Lagos. Use the map on pages 60-61 as far as Luz, then pick up Walk 1. Note that buses first call at the Salema crossroads (near the entrance to the Parque da Floresta golf resort, then turn down a steep hill to Salema village just under 2km further on, where they stop on the seafront.

Coastal footpaths always have great appeal, and this one is no exception. The moods of the sea, the play of light, a weaving coastline, the tang of salt, and secluded bays all help to etch them firmly into the memory. Fine views from the obelisk *(atalaia)* above Luz are one of the highlights of this walk, as is the egretry and the lighthouse at Ponta da Piedade. The interest at this point is the spectacular rugged coastline and the stacks around the coast.

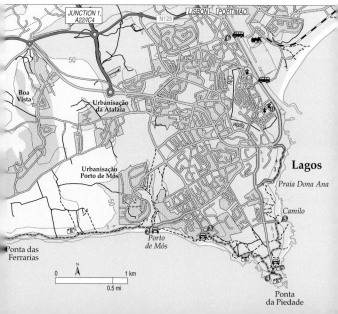

Stacks at Ponta da Piedade

Luz itself was a relatively small fishing village lying to the west of Lagos, but is rapidly developing as a tourist resort. The old centre is still intact, with some good restaurants and cafés. There are also fine beaches where you can swim or enjoy water sports such as windsurfing.

Interesting wild flowers, including orchids, can be found all along this part of the coast, and a description of these is given in the panel on pages 52-53.

Start the walk from the CAR PARK (**O**) by the sea at the eastern side of **Luz**: turn left towards the obelisk that you can see on the headland. Follow the cobbled road to the T-junction reached in under **1min**, where you turn right. At the second T-junction, a minute later, turn left, away from the shore. As the cobbled road ends, stay ahead on the rough track and follow it up the hillside. After **6min**, the track is leading you towards the obelisk, and you can see a path heading directly up the steepest part of the hillside. It is better *not* to take this path, but to use the curving path to the left. Erosion has made the footpaths difficult in parts, so some care is needed. The slow ascent at least gives you time to scan the hillside for flowers before you reach the OBELISK (**❶**; *P*1; **20min**). It's a good picnic spot, with some fine views to enjoy over Luz and along the coast, as well as along the valley inland.

Continue by following the track past the obelisk, heading in the direction of Lagos. The track dips through a hollow (**21min**), and back to the cliff tops. The walking soon becomes fairly level for a time, at a height of about 75m/250ft, and you gain views of Lagos ahead — as well as the lighthouse. Then you start the descent to Porto de Mós (**❷**; **48min**), taking care on this badly eroded track.

There is a selection of restaurant/cafés at **Porto de Mós** (**53min**) or an opportunity to picnic on the beach. To continue, head for the far side of the bay and the road out to Lagos. Walk up the road for under 400m/yds, until the wall of the complex on the right ends, and take the cobbled track off right. On meeting an asphalted crossroads a minute later, turn left uphill. Shortly, where a road (Travessa das Urzes) goes left, step over the low wall on the right, onto a road. Stay ahead for a few minutes, and you will come to a turning and parking area at the edge of the cliff. To the left of the wall ahead, you can pick up the coastal path again (❸; **1h08min**). Now the path undulates

A typical tiled façade in Lagos

slightly, before you eventually reach the LIGHTHOUSE at **Ponta da Piedade** (❹; **1h25min**).

Beyond the lighthouse, good views can be had if you have the energy to descend the steps to the landing stage, where boat trips from Praia Dona Ana land their passengers. Look carefully at the various stacks to identify the one used by the egrets as their breeding ground. It came as a surprise and delight to us to find that there are still regions of Algarve which remain unspoilt and where fine coastal walks are possible. Another such walk, further east, is described in Walk 12.

For the final stage into Lagos continue around the lighthouse to the CAR PARK (**1h27min**; restaurant/bar in season). Follow the Lagos road past the car park; then take the path on the right (**1h29min**). Wander as close to the cliffs as you like, then eventually come to another road (❺; **1h37min**) near a restaurant above the beach at **Camilo**. Since the paths on the far side of the road are now closed to the public, turn left here to join the Lagos road (**1h 40min**) and follow it to the right.

Keep ahead at the junction (**1h43min**; but divert right if you want to see the small resort and lovely beach at Praia Dona Ana, shown on page 6, and perhaps follow the coastal path to Lagos). You swing right through the CITY WALLS 10 minutes later. Follow the one-way system through the old town, turning left at the traffic lights. The MAIN SQUARE at **Lagos** (PRAÇA GIL EANES) soon comes into view (**2h03min**). The bus stops alongside the riverside road; the BUS STATION is upriver, opposite the marina.

THERE IS A WEALTH of wild flowers to be found along the whole of this coastal path from Lagos to Salema. Without doubt the best display is in the spring, but many plants, especially the cistus and other shrubs, do have a more prolonged flowering period. Limestone bluffs, eroded valleys offering protection for the plants from the wind and the salt, and deep-red coarse sandy soils are some of the different habitats which are to be seen. Orchids are particularly common in the limestone regions, and the short grass hides many bee orchids, including the bumblebee orchid, *Ophrys bombyliflora*, the yellow bee orchid, *O lutea*, and the mirror orchid, *O speculum* — as well as the tongue orchid, *Serapias parviflora*.

Less common are two charming narcissi — *N bulbocodium*, which resembles a small daffodil (photograph above), and the tiny jonquil,

Walk 2: LUZ • BURGAU • LUZ

See map page 55; see also photographs on pages 48 and 58

Distance: 9.5km/5.9mi; 2h10min *(allow at least 3h)*

Grade: ● easy. There is only one significant climb over a headland, and the footpaths, although stony in parts, are mostly good.

Equipment: See pages 41-42.

How to get there and return: 🚗 car or 🚌 bus from Lagos to/from Luz (Timetable 1). Journey time 15min. Motorists should follow signposting off left to Praia da Luz immediately on entering Luz, to a car park by the sea front (37° 5.240'N, 8° 43.548'W).

Short walk: Luz to Burgau (4.7km/2.9mi; 1h05min; ● grade as main walk). Follow the notes for the main walk to Burgau. Return from Burgau to Lagos by 🚌 bus (Timetable 1). Journey time 22min.

Longer walk: See Walk 1 for details of longer walks, including the option of walking between Luz and Salema.

This section of coastal path, westwards from Luz, is the easiest and the shortest. Although there are no sandy bays en route, Burgau awaits you, with its long stretch of beach — fine for swimming or just relaxing. See Walks 1 and 3 for more about the villages of Luz and Burgau.

Start the walk from the CAR PARK (**○**) at the sea front on the eastern side of **Luz**. Set out westward, away from the obelisk, along the PROMENADE. Turn right at the end of the promenade to pass a CHURCH on your right (**5min**) and then, almost immediately, take the first road left. Keep to the road; it becomes a track and then a path (after passing a sanitation plant on the left after about 10 minutes). Follow the path down left along the cliff top.

Be sure to watch out and avoid some DEEP HOLES on the right (**19min**). From here the path leads you left around a raised flat area, to end up at a slightly higher level (**23min**). As you reach a deep rocky bay (**26min**), cut

---

N gaditanus. Still on limestone, one interesting plant to see all year round is the dwarf fan palm, *Chamaerops humilis*. This is a native European palm; it rarely develops a stem, and the flowers are hidden in a dense cluster of leaves.

Common all along the cliffs, where it often forms neat mounds, is the yellow-flowered *Asteriscus maritimus*, which belongs to the daisy family. Cistus, too, are well represented, with the pink-flowered *Cistus albidus*, the white-flowered sage-leaved cistus, *Cistus salvifolius*, and *Halimium commutatum*, a yellow rock rose. An annual of the same family is the spotted rock rose, *Tuberaria guttata*, which has small yellow flowers with a dark brown centre.

The iris are so widespread that they are certain to be noticed — but possibly only after lunch, since *Iris sisyrinchium* opens its flowers only around mid-day. Two more to mention in this short list, both fairly common, are sweet alison, *Lobularia maritima*, with its fragrant small white flowers, and the blue-flowered tassel hyacinth, *Muscari comosum*.

inland to round it, keeping to the seaward side of the villas. Meet a gravel path and follow it to the left. When the gravel path ends, continue ahead on a path until (**38min**) you are on a path heading up the centre of the hill ahead. (Or you could skirt the base of the hill by taking a path to the right — *not left*.) Looking back, you can see the obelisk at Luz and, beyond it, the lighthouse near Lagos. Close at hand you should find fan-leaved palms and the much taller agaves (like those on page 63).

There is a short steep climb now, but new vistas open up as you reach the top (**41min**). Stay clear of the edge, as the cliff is very unstable at this point. Burgau lies on the far side of the windmill which you can see ahead and, on a clear day, it is possible to see all along the coastline to Sagres. Take care on the stony footpath, as you descend to continue on a wide path along the cliff edge.

This clear path leads directly towards Burgau, which you soon enter (**1h**). On reaching housing, the track runs into a road which you follow to descend to the shore. Coming into the heart of **Burgau** (**1h03min**), turn left towards the sea, passing toilets on your right, and continue right along the shore into the fishing harbour (**❶**).

Return to Luz the same way (**2h10min**) or, to end the Short walk, head up the narrow street from Burgau's harbour, to find the BUS STOP (**❸**).

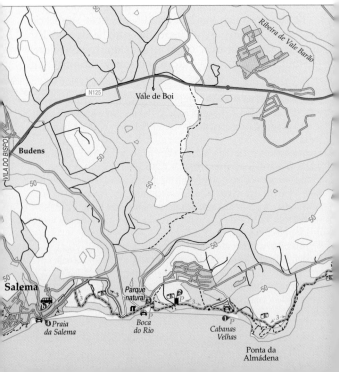

Walk 3: BURGAU • CABANAS VELHAS • BOCA DO RIO • SALEMA • BURGAU

Distance: 11km/6.8mi; 3h *(allow 4-5h)*

Grade: ● moderate. This coastal walk is full of headlands to negotiate, so there are quite a few ups and downs (550m/1800ft overall for the whole out-and-back walk). Some of the footpaths are stony and difficult.

Equipment: See pages 41-42.

Picnic suggestions *(no shade on any)*: Cabanas Velhas (35min-point in the walk, or drive there); isolated fort (50min-point in the walk or 15min on foot from Cabanas Velhas); Boca do Rio (30min on foot from Cabanas Velhas or drive there direct)

How to get there and return: 🚗 car or 🚌 bus from Lagos to/from Burgau (Timetable 1). Journey time 22min. By car, turn right by the bus shelter in Burgau and park on the wide road (37° 4.401'N, 8° 46.524'W).

Short walks

1 Burgau — Ponta da Almádena — Burgau (4.6km/2.9mi; 1h 10min). ● Easy, but there is some climbing and problems with stony paths. Follow the main walk for the first 35min, until you reach the small sheltered beach at Cabanas Velhas and a café/bar. Return the same way.

2 Burgau — Boca do Rio — Burgau (7.6km/4.7mi; 2h). ● Moderate. Use the notes for the main walk to go to the beach at Boca do Rio, where there are some Roman remains. Return the same way.

3 Burgau to Salema (5.5km/3.4mi; 1h27min). ● Moderate. Follow the main walk to Salema; return from there by bus (Timetable 2).

Burgau is one of the few fishing villages in Algarve whose core still retains its charm and character. The main street of the village runs down to the sea, where there are still some colourful fishing boats. This walk along the

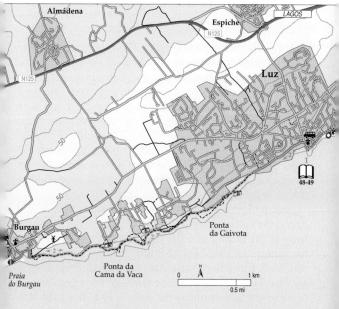

cliffs to Salema is very much like travelling a switchback — you climb the bluffs only to descend the other side. The two small beaches encountered en route make good resting places, although the beach at Cabanas Velhas all but disappears at high tide.

The bus stops at the corner of the wide road (near where there is room to park). **Start the walk** from the BUS STOP in **Burgau** (❹) by heading west along the wide street, with the sea over on your left. In around a minute, just past a WALLED SPORTS AREA, turn left into a narrower road. Follow this round to the right and continue ahead on a cliff path. Skirt the perimeter fence of a complex and wind up to a crossing path (**4min**), where you turn left uphill.

Once up on the HEADLAND (**6min**), you enjoy fine views back towards Lagos. The obelisk above Luz and the lighthouse near Lagos can both be seen. Follow the path by the cliff top as it dips down through a hollow. Over to the right farmhouses dot the barren countryside. There is another dip to cross and, as you rise again, the path runs into a rough track (**12min**). Keep ahead on the track by the coast, to get good views of the shingle beaches below.

Some **25min** along you can see Salema ahead and the Sagres headland in the distance. In **29min** the track descends through a cutting, to meet a crossing track a minute later. Turn sharp right here, but turn off this track in under a minute, to descend a path to a large expanse of sandy beach at **Cabanas Velhas** (❶; *P*3; **35min**), a good picnic spot.

Cross the beach to continue. There is an initial short steep climb but, by **39min**, you are back on the top again. Ahead you can see an old fort but, before you get there, there is a house to negotiate: as you meet the wall (**40min**), turn down right to keep alongside it and skirt the house (now on your left). Pick up the coastal path again beyond here and head towards the fort on the cliff edge. Keep right when there is a choice of paths, and reach the FORT in **50min** (❷; *P*3); the walls offer some shade for picnicking. Pass through the enclosure and out the other side to continue.

Stay with the coastal path as it swings to the right and starts into a steep descent towards the bay of Boca do Rio, lying at the mouth of a flat-bottomed valley. Just before the bottom of the valley (**56min**), the path joins a very rough track by a ruin on the left (note this carefully for the return). Turn left down to the riverside and cross over — on stepping stones unless the river is low. **Boca do Rio**

(❸; *P*3) is yet another — again shadeless — place to picnic on this walk. Inland is a good area for bird-watching. You'll notice signs of old fencing: there was once a fenced-off area here protecting an ancient Roman settlement, still awaiting excavation. Some of the remains are visible on the shore. The Boca do Rio is under threat of development, including a marina, despite being a conservation area.

Continue on the path leading up the cliff from the beach. Round the end of what's left of the perimeter fence and briefly meet the main track, uphill from Boca do Rio. As the main track sweeps inland, stay uphill on a rough track following the coast. As this track also starts to head

Two fine picnic spots on this walk: looking back towards the fort across the beach at Boca do Rio. Just out of sight, in the foreground, lie some Roman ruins.

On the coastal path between Burgau and Salema, looking towards Burgau

inland, look for the path off left along the cliff top (shown in the photograph above).

On approaching a house, the path (marked by stone arrows and cairns) swings downhill to the SALEMA ROAD (**1h20min**). Walk down to the seafront at **Salema**, with its beach, restaurants and cafés (**❹**; **1h27min**). *(To end Short walk 3, catch the bus in the village centre; **Ⓛ**)*

The main walk retraces steps to **Burgau** (**3h**).

Burgau (Longer walk 1-6 and Walks 2 and 3) is one of the Algarvian fishing villages that has retained its character despite all the touristic development further east along the splendid coast.

Walk 4: FIGUEIRA • INGRINA • ZAVIAL • FIGUEIRA

Distance: 12km/7.5mi; 3h05min *(allow around 5h)*

Grade: ● ⦂ ⦂ moderate-strenuous. Moderate undulations and an ascent of some 50m/160ft from Zavial. Some tricky cliff descents. Danger of vertigo on one short stretch during the descent to Praia das Furnas.

Equipment: See pages 41-42.

Picnic suggestions: beaches of Ingrina (1h33min on the walk) and Zavial (1h49min); both directly accessible by car; *no shade at either*

How to get there and return: 🚌 or 🚗 from Lagos to/from Figueira (Timetable 2). Journey time 20min. Check bus timetables locally, as more buses call at Budens and Salema than Figueira. (The Salema bus turns off the N125 just after Budens, at traffic lights. Alight immediately, where the bus goes left to Salema, and follow the road to Figueira.) Driving from Lagos on the N125, turn left for Salema, but keep ahead immediately for Figueira (as the Salema road goes left). Park on entering Figueira, before the bus shelter/toilets on the left (37° 4.401'N, 8° 46.524'W).

Short walk: Figueira — Praia das Furnas — Praia da Figueira — Figueira (6.4km/4mi; 1h40min). ● ⦂ Strenuous, with a possibility of vertigo around the 45min-mark). Follow the main walk to the 17min-point and turn left. Now use the map to reach Praia das Furnas (35min). Head to the seaward side of a buttress of rock on the left. To continue, pick up the Extended walk (below), from the 2h20min-point.

Extended walk: Figueira — Ingrina — Zavial — Praia das Furnas — Praia da Figueira — Figueira (13km/8.1mi; 3h35min). ● ⦂ Strenuous, with a possibility of vertigo around the 2h40min-mark. Follow the main walk to the 2h30min-point. Continue across Praia das Furnas, towards a bank of sand on the seaward side of a distinct buttress of rock. Start by taking a few steps up the sand bank, then scramble diagonally uphill to the right across the rough limestone. There is no distinct path, but head up left to the top just before reaching the edge of the cliff. Keep uphill when a cove comes into view ahead. At the top, move inland towards the centre of a saddle in the distance. Then descend diagonally right, to the inland edge of a hollow (2h43min). At this point the sea will be over to your right. Now head up the left flank of the mound ahead and contour round the hillside. Note the track below on the left and, soon, where a track leads from it seawards along the gully ahead, descend diagonally left to the junction of these tracks. On meeting the tracks turn right, seawards; then, almost immediately, turn left on a path and rise up the next mound. From the top of this mound, look across the dip ahead and note the path nearest the sea: this is your onward route. Descend to the inland side of the dip (keeping right at a fork) and, when you meet a crossing path, turn right towards the sea. In around a minute, where there is a collapsed stone wall on the right, fork left on a faint path rising diagonally along the hillside. Then pick up the path you spotted from the top of the mound — the one nearest the cliff edge — and continue uphill (2h57min). This path contours above the sea, then heads inland through a small fir tree plantation. Once clear of the trees, the masts above Figueira can be seen ahead. Then the path swings back to follow the coast and rises into an open area with good views of the coastline stretching ahead. Soon the ruined fort above Figueira beach comes into view. Eventually the path winds down the cliff to Praia da Figueira *(great care is needed on this steep and stony descent)*. Once at the bottom (3h13min), walk diagonally left, to locate the start of a trail. If the stream here is deep (it's usually just a trickle), head inland to locate stepping stones. Follow this trail (later a track) back to Figueira, where you emerge by the bus stop, just to the left of your starting point.

This circular walk explores some of the wildest country-side in Algarve, out in the far west. A large part of the hike follows the rugged coastline over numerous headlands, past quiet sandy bays. While swimmers will be attracted by these bays, the seas here are often rough, with a strong undertow, so choose a calm day. The beaches at Ingrina and Zavial have cafés which may open only at weekends and holidays out of season. This is a hearty, bracing walk. The climbs tend to be short and steep, but frequent. The landscape changes frequently, too — with coastal views one moment and wild countryside the next.

Start out from the BUS SHELTER in **Figueira** (**O**) by continuing west along the road, with the main part of the village to your right. Ignore a track on the left immediately. *(This is where the Extended walk comes back into Figueira.)* Just after crossing a small BRIDGE (under **5min**), turn left on a narrow road. Ignore a track up left six minutes later. A lone ruined windmill up on the right surveys a rolling countryside chequered with pockets of cultivation. Keep ahead at DIAGONAL CROSS-TRACKS (**a**; **17min**). *(The return route from Praia das Furnas joins from the left here.)* The road approaches a COMPLEX OF RED-ROOFED BUILDINGS and

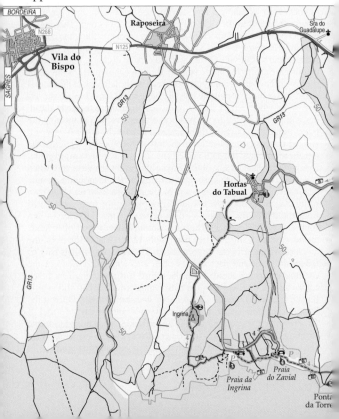

swings right to skirt round the complex (**20min**), passing the entrance on the left. Rise to reach a crossing track and keep ahead to pass a white house below on the left (**27min**; photograph overleaf). Agaves line the route for a short distance, as the road levels out. In **30min** Hortas do Tabual comes into view ahead. In a landscape of hills and hollows, the road dips and then rises, finally swinging left to make a U-turn back towards Hortas.

Entering **Hortas do Tabual** (➊), stay ahead into the village as the road sweeps right. Take the next right turn. Cross the main village road and continue ahead, past a WATER TROUGH on the right, to the RAPOSEIRA/ZAVIAL ROAD (**46min**). Keep ahead now on a track that descends into a small valley, ignoring a right fork into a field. Then rise up to another track (**55min**), which ends at a house on the left. Turn right along this track, away from the house; then, in a little over a minute, as the track bends left, keep ahead on a field track. This faint track undulates beneath a line of TELEGRAPH POLES which lead towards a cluster of BUILDINGS — where you are heading. When a track joins from the right (**1h02min**), continue ahead to the RAPOSEIRA/INGRINA ROAD (**1h05min**).

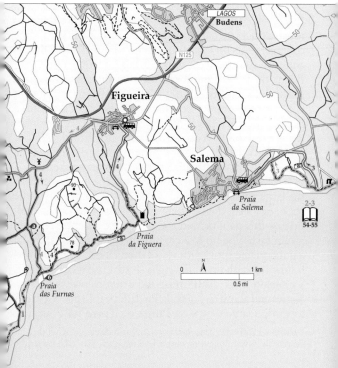

Turn right, cross the road and head seawards down the road to the left, between the buildings opposite. This reverts to a wide track in two minutes. Just over three minutes later, stay ahead on a field track as you approach the entrance to the neglected-looking old **Ingrina** CAMP-SITE (**2**). Then keep right as this track forks and reverts to path. Head due south towards the sea, with the campsite over to your left. The track climbing the distant hillside ahead is your ongoing route. Skirt to the right of a clump of EUCALYPTUS TREES (**1h13min**). The path leads through the *Cistus* to an open area. Veer left to meet the path coming from the campsite (**1h18min**), where you continue to the right. Ignore a track off left (**1h22min**) and start to descend. A minute later, at a T-junction, keep round to the left. There are some magnificent coastal views to enjoy now, as Ingrina comes into full view. At a fork, keep left downhill, to a surfaced ROAD (**1h30min**). Turn left on the road, then either keep ahead to the Ingrina road and turn right, or take a path off right (before a ruin), to cross the **Praia da Ingrina** (**3**; *P*4; **1h33min**). If you've no picnic, the café here is even open at times in winter, especially at weekends.

Leave Praia da Ingrina by crossing the café car park and follow the path along the cliff top. The path dips down to touch a track, then continues up ahead, initially with some concrete posts on the left. Descend to a track (**1h 38min**) and cross straight over* on a path heading towards a house. Below the house, you rejoin the cliff route and come to a junction above Zavial. The path to the left is more difficult, with tree roots underfoot; the one to the right demands a head for heights, but is the easier descent. *Take care when using either route.* You reach **Praia do Zavial** (**4**; *P*4; **1h49min**), another possible picnic spot, at the right of the café — which also usually opens on winter weekends.

To continue, head seawards across the beach, towards the large rocks at the base of the cliff. Scramble over the rocks to locate the ongoing path at the base of the cliff. Follow this path behind and above the beaches. A stony ascent takes you up to a crossing path (**1h59min**); this is a good picnic spot, with views over Zavial. Turn left and follow the path up to the right — to a rise where there is a crossing track (**2h03min**) and extensive views back to Sagres and ahead to Ponte da Piedade near Lagos. Go right towards a large CAIRN on **Ponta da Torre** (**5**), but fork

*There is a cliff-edge path further on, but it is dicey. To avoid the cliff descent to Zavial altogether, turn left on the track, then take the road.

Agaves line the route for a short distance, as the road levels out near a white house (about 27 minutes into the walk).

left downhill immediately. (The curious might wish to divert right to the cairn, thought to have been a watch-tower at one time.) Keep left as a track joins from the right, but stay ahead as the main track sweeps left inland (**2h06min**). Fork left, then right, to meet a cross-track a few minutes later. Keep right again, to continue in the same direction, on a now quite stony path/track which rounds a shallow gully.

When you come to a wide crossing path, with a small cairn down to the right, at the edge of the cliff (**2h15min**), turn left (north). Soon you will see a white house on a mound ahead and the white mass of Salema along the coast to the right. In just over two minutes, stay with the main path*, which forks off right, and head for the mouth of Praia das Furnas cove. When a wall blocks the way, go left. About a minute later, fork right to pass through a gap in the wall. Start into the gradual descent to the cove, and do not be tempted to turn right down any of the many fishermen's paths. Praia das Furnas comes into view, and the path crosses a rocky area, becoming clear again as it continues diagonally towards the beach. Vertigo may be a problem for some on a short stretch where the path traverses close to the cliff edge. Do not cut down to the beach too soon; keep a steady course towards the back of the beach. You reach the **Praia das Furnas** (❻) in **2h30min**. *(The Extended walk carries on from this point.)*

To head back inland to Figueira, follow the stony track leading from the back of the beach. This crosses a stream bed to reach a T of tracks. Turn right and cross back over the stream bed to continue. Keep ahead, ignoring a track off right, until you reach the DIAGONAL CROSS-TRACKS (❹) first encountered at the 17min-point on the outward route (**2h48min**). Turn right here, then turn right again on the road, back to the BUS SHELTER in **Figueira** (❶; **3h05min**).

*To bypass Praia das Furnas, keep heading north. At the fork 300m/yds past the track off right to the white house, keep right on the main track. Descend to the beach track and turn left, back to the 17min-point.

Walk 5: MEXILHOEIRA NATURE WALK

Distance: 8km/5mi; 1h40min *(allow 2h30min)*

Grade: ● easy, mostly level walking on tracks; red/yellow waymarking

Equipment: See pages 41-42.

How to get there and return: 🚐, 🚌 or 🚆 to/from Mexilhoeira Grande
🚐: alight at Mexilhoeira Grande, the first station east of Portimão
(Timetable 9)
🚌: Portimao-Lagos bus to Mexilhoeira Grande(not in the timetables,
but daily departures, hourly (www.frotazul-algarve.pt). Alight on the
N125 and take the lane on the seaward side of the road signed 'ESTAÇÃO'.
🚆: drive the N125 to Mexilhoeira Grande, between Lagos and Portimão
(the 25.5km-point on Car tour 1). (If travelling via the A22/IC4
motorway, leave at Junction 3 and turn left on reaching the N125.) The
lane to the station, on the seaward side of the N125, is signed 'ESTAÇÃO'.
Park outside the station (37° 9.265'N, 8° 36.587'W).

Shorter walk (5.4km/3.4mi; 1h10min). ● Easy; follow the main walk
to the 35min-point. Turn left here then pick up the notes from the
1h10min-point to return to the start.

This walk, which starts and finishes on the platform of
a small railway station, explores some wetlands near
the sea. It is a refreshing countryside walk for all to enjoy
but will be especially interesting for bird-watchers. The
highlights for us were spoonbills and flamingos. An information board on the railway platform shows the route of
this easily followed walk.

Start the walk at **Mexilhoeira Grande** RAILWAY
STATION (**O**) by walking into the station and turning left
to cross the railway line at the crossing point at the end of
the platform. Join the track on the other side of the railway
line and turn right — noticing that you are following RED/
YELLOW WAYMARKS. Continue ahead with the railway line
on your right, to reach a crossroads (**❶**; **5min**). The road
on your left here is the return route.

Continue ahead, now on a narrow road, to reach a bend
(**14min**) and follow the bend around to the left, ignoring
the track off to the right. The views start to open up a little,
and soon Lagos and Ponte da Piedade come into view over
to the right. You come to a JUNCTION (**❷**) in **35min**. *(The
Shorter walk turns left here, back to the station.)* Keep ahead
very briefly, then turn right to start a 2km-long circuit
around an area of pools, diches and dykes, where some of
the bird life may be seen. Turn left on reaching the seafront
and left again when you come to the small beach, heading
inland to complete the circuit.

Now retrace your steps briefly then turn right at the
junction (**❷**; **1h10min**). The gentle uphill walking here
almost comes as a surprise, but as you climb and gain a little
altitude you can enjoy some views of Monchique, Foia and

Flamingoes on the Mexilhoeira nature walk — at about the 1h10min-point

Picota. On descending back towards the railway track, you pass the Arocha Life Nature Centre (❸) on the left (www. arocha.pt). The centre is open to the public on Thursday mornings (including bank holidays). For bird ringing demonstrations and bird tours telephone 282 968 8380 (Groups of 10 or more ring in advance.) A list of birds seen that week is pinned on the board outside. Continue along the track to reach the outward track (❶) and railway line (**1h35min**). Turn right back to the RAILWAY STATION (◎).

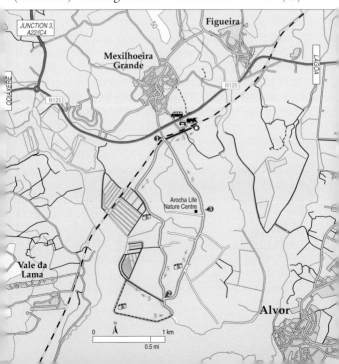

Walk 6: BARÃO SÃO JOÃO CIRCUIT

Distance: 7.3km/4.6mi; 1h50min *(allow 2h30min)*

Grade: ● easy. There is just a little climbing in the first part of the walk — all in shade. Red/yellow waymarking

Equipment: See pages 41-42.

How to get there and return: ⛟ only accessible by car. Barão São João is a short detour away from Espiche, the 48km-point on Car tour 1. Otherwise, follow the A22/IP4 motorway to the very western end and turn right towards Bensafrim. Drive through the village and turn right along the road signposted to Barão São João. Just over 4km further on, as you enter Barão, dog-leg through by turning left, then right. After 100m turn left again, into a parking area (37° 8.326'N, 8° 46.567'W). This is a good parking spot for both exploring the village and starting the walk. There is more parking at the entrance to the park itself (37° 8.374'N, 8° 46.778'W), but it shortens the walk and you could miss out on the village.

Tucked away deep in the countryside, seemingly in the back of beyond, Barão São João is a surprisingly lively, colourful village with a pedestrianised area and a number of coffee shops. Locals flock here in summer to enjoy the numerous picnic sites in the nearby woodland. This influx has brought a touch of prosperity and added life to this otherwise sleepy place.

The walk takes place in a section of *mata nacional* (national forest), and *parque de merendas* (picnic park). In truth, however, 'forest' as used in this case refers to fairly open woodland, with a mix of eucalyptus, acacia and native umbrella pines. There are a number of wind turbines in this region and sometimes the blades can be seen above the forest canopy — and at one point the walk passes close to one.

Start the walk from the PARKING AREA (**O**) by continuing along the main road in the same direction as you arrived. Soon turn right uphill on a road signposted 'MATA NACIONAL' to reach the PARK ENTRANCE and large CAR PARK (**❶; 7min**). You pick up RED/YELLOW WAYMARKS here and continue ahead on this wide track, still in steady ascent. Ignoring any tracks to the left, rise up to a junction (**13min**), were you *do* turn left, for the moment following the sign 'PR1 LGS' (Percurso Pedestre Pedra do Galo). The park RANGER'S HOUSE (**❷**) is reached very shortly, and the track turns right alongside it. There are a number of picnic areas scattered around nearby, and you pass through one of them a couple of minutes later. Ignore a fork further on leading down to another picnic area (Pedro do Galo) and keep right. The track takes a sharp left bend shortly so that you walk around the picnic area which can be seen again down to the left.

Sand crocus, gladioli and blue scilla flowers deck the way

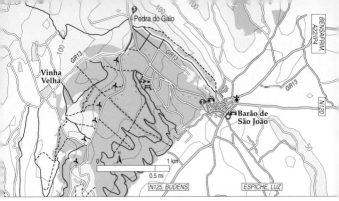

in spring as you continue to follow this track until meeting a rough CROSSING TRACK (**43min**). Turn right uphill now, on this stony track, and notice the wind turbine coming into view. Enjoy this long straight stretch, especially the SMALL POND decorated with an oversize stone fish on the left, before reaching a T-JUNCTION BETWEEN TWO WIND TURBINES (**56min**).

Turn right here, to pass a turbine on the left and then a second one even closer on the left. The track heading sharply back to the left quickly reached (**1h10min**) is part of the GR13 Algarve Way. Then you come to a wide diagonal crossing track (**1h14min**) — your return route. But first walk ahead to the goal of the waymarked walk: **Pedra do Galo** (❸), a Stone Age menhir, from where you have fine views over the surrounding countryside. Return to the cross-track and now keep straight ahead, passing the 'PR1 LGS' SIGN of the outward route (**1h24min**). You're back at the park entrance a few minutes later and then your car by the main road in **Barão** (❍; **1h36min**).

This small pond, passed at about 50min into the walk, is decorated with a stone fish

Walk 7: FÓIA ROAD • MADRINHA • PÉ DO FRIO • CHILRÃO • FÓIA ROAD

Distance: 11km/6.9mi; 2h50min *(allow 4-5h)*

Grade: ● moderate-strenuous. There is a descent of 375m/1230ft in the first part which has to be regained on the return. The footpaths and tracks used are generally good underfoot.

Equipment: See pages 41-42.

How to get there and return: 🚌 only accessible by car. From Monchique follow the signs for Fóia. Some 6km from Monchique (200m past the *miradouro*, at the point where the road bends right), park down the second of two tracks close together on the left, in an open area with some ruined buildings (37° 18.579'N, 8° 36.461'W).

Shorter walks (both are ●)

1 **Fóia road — Madrinha — Fóia road** (1.8km/1.1mi; 22min). Easy grade, but rough underfoot in places. Follow the main walk to enjoy the views from the summit of Madrinha. Then return the same way.

2 **Fóia road — Pé do Frio — Chilrão — Fóia road** (10.3km/6.4mi; 2h42min). Grade and notes as for main walk, but omit the climb to Madrinha.

The *serras* which make up the most northerly part of Algarve are generally dull and monotonous. Their schistose composition generates an acid soil which supports a uniform *matos* consisting mainly of gum cistus, *Cistus ladanifer*. But the Serra de Monchique is altogether different. Its greater height gives it an imposing presence, and its granite composition favours a more varied and interesting flora. This area provides the most demanding walking in Algarve.

After first climbing the nearby summit of Madrinha (803m/2634ft) to enjoy the views, this walk then descends its western slopes, to visit two small villages before circling back by a different route. It starts 200m/yds past the viewpoint near the top of Fóia signposted 'Fonte/ Miradouro'. It's not unusual to find one or two locals here, offering to sell home-made produce to passers-by, including honey and *medronho*, a spirit made from the fruit of the strawberry tree (see panel opposite).

Start out at the PARKING PLACE (**O**): with your back to the road, go west down the wide track, keeping to the north (right) of Madrinha. Stay left on the wide track at a fork in under **3min**, now joining the **Algarve Way**. Ignore a track off left but, at the top of the rise (**7min**), fork left uphill to the SUMMIT of **Madrinha** (**❶**; **11min**), marked by a trig point and a fire-watch station. *(Stay right downhill for Shorter walk 2)*. This is one of the region's finest viewpoints: given a clear day, it is possible to pick out a whole host of landmarks stretching the full breadth of Algarve.

Walk back down to the main track (**15min**) and turn

STRAWBERRY TREE

left. *(But for Shorter walk 1, turn right and retrace steps back to your car.)* Walk to the right of FOUR WIND TURBINES and, just short of the fifth, descend to the left on a narrower track (**②**). (You have now left the Algarve Way.) Ignoring any side tracks, keep descending, with the summit of Picos close by on the left and views to Pé do Frio on the right.

Just over 100m short of a ROAD, be sure to keep left, to reach the road at a junction (**50min**). This is the road to Pé do Frio, but the old route is more scenic, so cross the road and take the track to the right, descending parallel with the road. Stay right at the fork reached two minutes later, to enjoy good views across the valley to Pé do Frio. Where the track swings down left (**54min**), keep ahead on a path, past a small house up to the right. The field track/path descends, crosses a gully, and bends left. Step round any animal barriers that may be across the field track/path. At

Strawberry tree (Arbutus unedo)

AS ITS NAME indicates, you eat only one! The fruits of the strawberry tree are unpalatable, but they make a splendid *aguardente*, a firewater called *medronho*.

The tree flowers in September and October, and it is at this time that the previous year's fruit starts to ripen and really resembles a strawberry. Only then is it ready for collection.

The fruit is fermented in wooden barrels to produce alcohol with only enough water to cover the mass. The natural yeasts already present on the fruit start the fermentation. Mud is used to seal the barrels, with a tube for escaping gases, to protect the alcohol from further oxidation.

By January the fermentation is usually complete, and it is ready for distillation. This process uses a specially-designed copper kettle, which is heated over a wood fire. A medium-sized kettle will handle about 100 kilos of the fermented brew, but the mass needs to be stirred by hand to prevent burning, until it is necessary to fit the tubes ready for distillation. A slow and steady distillation rate gives the best results and produces *medronho* which is about 90% proof. Your visit to Algarve will not be complete without sampling some *medronho* at one of the bars in Caldas…

Rhododendron ponticum, *with the Monchique hills in the background*

1h06min turn right at the junction, to enter the main part of **Pé do Frio** (❸), the hamlet shown on page 49. Turn left on meeting the road less than a minute later.

Chilrão soon comes into sight. It too is just a scattering of farm houses and has no shops. Keep on the road to pass **Chilrão** (❹; **1h25min**), and stay right at the road junction two minutes later. Ignore the track joining from the left after 130m/yds, but take the track ascending to the right about 50m/yds further on (opposite a track off left, at a point where the road is itself starting to bend away to the right).

Slip into low gear as the uphill section now gets underway, with good views on the left. Stay ahead at the

Caldas de Monchique, a well-restored village

diagonal crossing track (**1h45min**). Seven minutes later, fork right, where a track continues ahead. Stay with the track as the route describes a U-turn to the right, back towards Fóia, with a valley on the right. A couple of minutes beyond the point where the track widens out by some pylons, be sure to go sharp left on the main track (**2h06min**). From this sharp bend there are some spectacular views, especially towards the steep terraces just below Madrinha. You can also see a zigzag of tracks below Fóia; this is where our route will eventually take us. Take another sharp turn (**2h09min**), this time to the right, where a track continues ahead. Swing left two minutes later, then keep ahead (**2h21min**).

Terracing brings a neat order and grace to the steep hillsides, as you continue steadily uphill along the main track. As you leave the shade of a EUCALYPTUS WOOD (**2h 23min**), fork right on a woodland track, rejoining the Algarve Way (**5**). It becomes clear that you are walking a horseshoe circuit around the valley down to your right. Pé do Frio and Chilrão can both be seen below. At a fork in the track, where the Algarve Way goes right (**2h41min**), keep left uphill. All along this section there are fine views down over old terraces and farm clusters. The track rises to the ROAD (**2h49min**). The PARKING PLACE where the walk began is just to the right (**○**; **2h50min**).

Walk 8: MONCHIQUE • FÓIA • MONCHIQUE

Distance: 10.6km/6.6mi; 2h20min *(allow about 4h)*

Grade: ● moderate. Monchique is situated at an elevation of around 400m/1300ft, which still leaves 500m/1640ft of climbing before you reach the top of Fóia. Although the route is fairly direct, the going is rarely very steep, which makes the walk less strenuous than it might appear. The walk is straightforward enough to be navigable in cloud.

Equipment: See pages 41-42.

How to get there and return: 🚗 car or 🚌 bus from Portimão to/from Monchique (Timetable 3). Journey time 32-45min. Travelling by car, park in Monchique's main square (37° 19.088'N, 8° 33.354'W) or at the viewpoint on the right, as you enter the square.

Short walks

1 **Monchique — Nossa Senhora de Desterro — Monchique** (1.6km/1mi; 21min). ● Easy; no special equipment needed. Follow the main walk to the ruins of the 17th-century convent; return the same way.

2 **Fóia to Monchique** (5.6km/3.5mi; 1h20min). ● Grade as main walk. Take a taxi from Monchique to the top of Fóia (8km) and use the map to walk back down. Start out from the car park, by heading down to the nearest cluster of aerials and dishes, to find the minor surfaced road leading off to the left, signposted to Restaurante Jardim das Oliveiras.

A t 902m/2960ft, Fóia is the highest peak in Algarve, but the summit — adorned as it is with clusters of radio and television masts, a concrete obelisk, restaurant *(which may be closed in winter, even on weekends)* and gift shops — is not especially attractive. However, the views are truly panoramic and, should you be fortunate to choose a clear day, you can see Sagres on the southern side and out to Cape St Vincent — one of the most westerly tips of mainland Europe; to the north the mountain ranges south of Lisbon are visible. Monchique itself seems to offer little of interest as you arrive in the main square, but you will discover the real character of the place in the narrow streets where the walk begins.

The walk starts at the main square in **Monchique**, the LARGO 5 DE OUTUBRO (**○**), where you alight from the bus. Leave the square from the top right-hand corner from where you entered, along the narrow cobbled street to the right called RUA DO PORTO FUNDO. In less than a minute turn left into a narrow alley (TRAVESSA DAS GUERREIRAS) and climb the shallow steps, to cross a narrow street (**2min**) and continue upwards. At the next junction, reached in less than a minute, keep to the right initially, then swing left (RUA DO CASTELO). You're now on the **Algarve Way**, which has come up from Monchique by a slightly different route. Still climbing, swing right in **4min** (LARGO DO CONVENTO) and continue in a steep ascent on CAMINHO DO CONVENTO. In **6min**, where the road goes down to the right, keep ahead to join an old trail. This

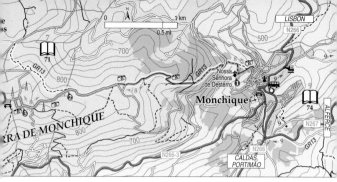

leads past a WATER PUMPING STATION and a SHRINE on the wall, both on the left. Good views soon open up back towards Monchique to the left and across to Picota on the right, where you can see the trig point and the fire-watch tower (both visited in Walk 9). Ignore another old trail which sweeps off to the right (**9min**) and continue ahead to the ruined Franciscan convent dating from 1623, **Nossa Senhora de Desterro** (❶; **11min**). *(Short walk 1 turns back here.)*

Go right as you reach the convent, taking a path which leads directly uphill through the woodland. Cork oaks provide shade as you follow the path which rises to meet an old trail (**13min**). Turn left now to leave the oak woodland and start in a steeper ascent. The trail swings left and rises to pass between crash barriers, onto a surfaced road (**17min**), where you turn left. But be sure to turn right almost immediately, onto a rough track. Just about a minute up this track (**19min**), take the path which leads off to the left. Woodlands shade the way as you climb steadily, to run into a woodland track (**22min**), where you continue to the right uphill. Scents of pine and eucalyptus mingle as you tread softly on the carpet of forest litter.

The open countryside below Fóia. Some of the flora you can expect to see on this walk in early season are the small funnel-shaped lilac flowers of Romulea bulbocodium, *blue* Scilla monophyllos — *a plant easily distinguished by its single leaf, and the broad-leaved* Epipactis helleborine.

On meeting the next track (**27min**), on a bend, follow it straight ahead, uphill. Keep steadily uphill, ignoring tracks right and left. When the track bends sharply right (**35min**) there are good open views over to the right. Two minutes later, bend left and continue rising above and around the valley on the left. Ignore a minor track down left and reach a track running diagonally to the left (**48min**), just before the track becomes more level. Turn up *right* here on a very rough track.

Fóia comes into view ahead as you rise to meet a road (**50min**), just beyond a bend. Go right along the narrow road towards the summit. There is as much interest in the immediate landscape (photograph page 73) as in the distant views. Terraces woven into steep hillsides suggest a sleep of centuries, isolated farms shimmer in the sun, and the sense of tranquillity is enhanced by the sound of distant cowbells. About halfway along the road, the Algarve Way heads off to the right (**❷**) — offering a different, slightly longer approach to the summit (see map), or linking up with Walk 7 after 2.5km.

After enjoying the views from the SUMMIT of **Fóia** (**❸**; **1h12min**), retrace your steps to the shops, restaurant and

car parking area. Take a break for refreshments, then return the same way to **Monchique** (**❍**; **2h20min**).

The cork oak is an important feature of the Algarve landscape. This cork collection point is encountered at the 42min-point in Walk 9.

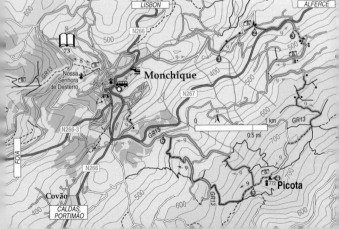

Walk 9: MONCHIQUE — PICOTA CIRCUIT

See map and photograph opposite

Distance: 12km/7.5mi; 3h15min *(allow about 5h)*

Grade: ● moderate. The ascent of 400m/1300ft is mostly gradual and the footpaths and tracks used are mainly good underfoot.

Equipment: See pages 41-42.

How to get there and return: 🚗 car or 🚌 bus to/from Monchique (Timetable 3; journey time 35-45min). Motorists could park as for Walk 8 (37° 19.088'N, 8° 33.354'W) or at the heliport at the start of the walk.

Shorter walk: Monchique — Picota — Monchique (7.5km/4.7mi; 2h30min). ● Grade as main walk. Start out by walking south from Monchique on the Portimão road for about three minutes, then turn left down a cobbled road, passing a tap on the left. Use the map to follow the Algarve Way/GR13 and climb to Picota, then return by a different route, following the main walk from the 1h47min-point.

Picota is the twin of Fóia, peaking a little lower (at 774m/2540ft). Monchique lies in the valley between the two. Picota provides interesting walking, with the added bonus of tranquillity on the summit. Botanically it is possibly the more interesting mountain, although the eucalyptus plantations to its north do nothing to help in this respect, since their thirsty roots denature the soil.

Start the walk from the main square in **Monchique**, the LARGO 5 DE OUTUBRO (**○**): head out along the Lisbon road (N266), passing the FISH MARKET and HELIPORT on the right. Just past the heliport take the right fork downhill (**6min**), signposted 'CRUZ DOS MADEIROS', to descend a narrow road past a sports ground over to the left. On coming to a HAMLET (300m/yds from the fork), go right again along the road through the hamlet. As this road reverts to track (**10min**) stay ahead through the cork oak woods. Pass a track entering from the right and stay along the main track as it bends left to meet a tarmac road.

Turn right here to continue downhill and cross the BRIDGE over the river. Almost immediately, as the road rises, fork left into a WALLED TRACK (**①**). The track leads to a house called QUINTA BOLAO (**25min**); continue along the right-hand side of the house on the track. Then fork right uphill, to continue alongside the wall on the right. Soon, you are back in a walled-in path and can enjoy views over this fertile valley.

After rising steeply, the path runs into a road (**30min**) and passes a farm on the left. Rise to join a narrow road coming in from the right less than a minute later. Keep right at the fork almost immediately and stay with the road to climb back into cork oak woodland. The CORK COLLECTION POINT shown opposite is passed just before you reach a junction (**42min**); turn right here, up a disused track, passing an OLD FARM (**❷**) on the left. This takes you to the Alferce road just over two minutes later.

Turn left, past the BUS SHELTER, and in under one minute fork right uphill along a very narrow (unsigned) road. Stay on the road, which bends right. In four minutes start into a bend to the left (**50min**), then keep ahead past a house on the right — on a NARROW PATH (**❸**; stone paved in parts) which leads uphill through terraces. Stay up this path, ignoring a path off left, and rise onto a crossing path five minutes later. Go right here, across the front of the OLD FARM BUILDING on the left. The narrow footpath leads past an old stone building (possibly once a WATERMILL) and under a STONE ARCH before going sharply uphill to the left. Turn right on meeting the tarmac road in a few minutes. Soon pass a road off left to a farm as the road you are on now contours along the hillside with open views across the valley to Monchique and Foia. You rise to pass a FARM WITH SILOS on the left (**1h06min**).

When you reach another road (**1h13min**), turn left and climb steeply uphill, but in just over a minute watch for an optional footpath off left through a small eucalyptus plantation. Otherwise, stay along the road and follow it in a bend to the left and note where the optional path soon emerges from the left. Stay with the road for a further seven minutes, then head right when the road forks (**1h25min**). Go right again less than a minute later, on a track (initially surfaced with concrete).

Keep ahead along the hillside, passing a farm on the left, where the way becomes a rough woodland track. Follow the main track which eventually swings left, then soon heads right just past an old building on the left. Almost immediately, ignore the rough track going left uphill, but turn left at a crossing track (just beyond a modern house downhill to the right). This track climbs steadily to a T-junction. Go right here, on a more level woodland track, and ignore a track joining from the right some 200m/yds further on (part of the **Algarve Way**; **1h48min**). Keep ahead for a further 30m/yds to a crossing track (marked by an ORANGE ARROW on bedrock), and turn right. This track reverts to a trail waymarked with ORANGE DOTS.

Turn left as you meet a road (**1h56min**), now heading for the summit, which soon comes into view. The climb is quite steep; clamber over the rocks to reach the TRIG POINT and FIRE-WATCH STATION on **Picota** (**❹; 2h08min**).

There are fantastic views towards Fóia and the convent passed in Walk 8. The Barragem da Bravura can be seen in the south, as well as Portimão and Lagos on the coast.

Leave the summit on the far side of the watch-tower from your first approach, following ORANGE DOTS. Descend carefully over the granite rocks, heading for a small saddle and path (roughly 250°; Monchique is over to your right). Soon after joining this path, look for a woodland track downhill to the right (❺; **2h15min**), way-marked with an ORANGE ARROW; this takes you downhill through a plantation. *(The Alternative descent on the GR 13 Algarve Way goes straight on at this point; see footnote below.*)* Ignore minor tracks off your route and, when you come to a T-junction, turn right. Keep left downhill on meeting a narrow road. When you meet another road (on a bend; **2h36min**), turn right to continue downhill. Just after rejoining the Algarve Way, at a 'T' of roads (❻; **2h46min**), turn left.

A few minutes later you reach the main ALFERCE ROAD, where you again turn left. Just before the ROUNDABOUT on the main MONCHIQUE/PORTIMÃO ROAD, turn sharp right to enter a WALLED-IN ROAD (❼; **2h57min**) which leads back in the direction from which you have just come, but at a lower level. Just after the road ends three minutes later (past a house), turn left on a track towards another house. Continue up the path to the left of this house, heading towards Monchique. Stay uphill as the path bends right towards some apartments. Rise onto a cobbled road and go left. As you come to a WATER TAP on the right, turn left to the MAIN ROAD (**3h10min**). Turn right here, back to the MAIN SQUARE in **Monchique** (❶; **3h14min**).

***Alternative, waymarked descent on the Algarve Way** (adds 10min to the overall timing for the walk). Keep straight ahead at the 2h15min-point (❺), where signposts indicate that it is 550m back to the top of Picota, and that the way ahead is the red/white waymarked Algarve Way and also waymarked in red/yellow as an AlgarveTourism route. Follow the main route, a rough woodland track, round to the right and downhill. Descend to a narrow road (with a 'Picota' sign) and go right. At the next T-junction turn left and keep right when a road joins from the left. At a fork (with a ruin on the right), go left downhill, past the gate to a house on the left. Your narrow road swings left but, almost immediately, take a path off to the right. The path, well used, paved in parts and marked with occasional ORANGE BLOBS, meanders downhill through woodland. The path broadens to a minor field track and descends to a T-junction: turn right on this new track. Meeting another narrow road, turn left past a brick red-coloured house. At the next junction turn left to join the main walk at the 'T' of roads (❻), described above. Follow the main walk from the 2h46min-point to the end.

Walk 10: ILHA DO ROSÁRIO CIRCUIT

Distance: 7.5km/4.7mi; 1h34min *(allow 2h30min)*

Grade: ● easy, mainly level walking along a watercourse *(levada)*

Equipment: See pages 41-42.

How to get there and return: 🚗 only by car. From the Silves round-about, take the N124 towards Monchique for 4.2km Turn left into the Mira-Rio restaurant car park, just after a sharp right bend (37° 11.214'N, 8° 29.245'W). Mira-Rio permits parking and using their path to get to the *levada;* we always buy a drink or snack there as a 'thank you'. If the gate to the *levada* is locked, go back 0.4km along the road and park tucked in where a field track leads down to the *levada* at the 8min-point (see map).

Shorter version of the main walk (6.4km/4mi; 1h12min). ● Easy. Park in the small lay-by on the left, 3.9km/2.4mi from Silves roundabout, just before two tracks turn off left and the road bends sharp right (37° 11.189'N, 8° 29.186'W). Take the downhill track next to the lay-by. In under a minute, you will reach the point where the track crosses the watercourse. Turn left on the path alongside this *levada* and pick up the main walk from the 8min-point. Leave the walk at the same point on your return.

Bounded by two rivers, and a haven of peace and solitude, Rosário might as well be an island — as its name 'Ilha' suggests. This delightful bucolic walk follows a watercourse *(levada)* around the hillside, trapped between cliffs and the river, then completes the circuit of the hill by quiet country lanes. One of the pleasures of this walk is the ease by which you escape to landscapes quite unlike any others in Algarve. Since this walk is handily situated close to Silves, you could try Walk 11 in the morning, have lunch in Silves, explore the town, and then enjoy this stroll in the afternoon.

Start the walk by descending the path to the left of the MIRA-RIO RESTAURANT (●) to the *levada* below. Cross the watercourse and turn left along the adjacent footpath. At this point the **Ribeira de Odelouca** is quite close on the right, and the path passes housing on the left. Orange groves are a feature as the *levada* contours the hillside. A field track crosses the watercourse (❸; **8min**): the Shorter version joins here, and this is a more direct return route for the return, as it emerges near the Mira-Rio restaurant. A roughly-surfaced narrow road crosses less than four minutes later (**11min**). The road remains alongside the *levada* for a while, and you soon cross it again. A small PUMPING STATION (❶) on the left marks the **16min**-point; the return route rejoins the *levada* here. The elevated path gives good views over the river, a peaceful setting where you may see some birds. After **24min**, cross left over the *levada,* to continue along the other side, then cross back again less than two minutes later. At this point make a diversion to a rocky promontory at the CONFLUENCE (❷)

78

The levada *(watercourse) and the*
Ribeira de Odelouca

of the **Odelouca** and **Arade**
rivers. This is a favourite
haunt of the local fishermen, a great viewpoint and
ideal picnic stop.

Back on the *levada*, as
you approach the narrow
surfaced road crossed
earlier (**31min**; by a house
on the right), the path
crosses back to the left-hand
side of the watercourse.
Around two minutes later,
you enjoy views back to the
river confluence. Then
Silves comes into view
ahead (**42min**). As the
levada swings away from
the river, you might like to
take a path downhill to a
riverside CAFÉ/BAR (❸;
open all year round, but
perhaps only on weekends
out of season). Otherwise,
keep ahead as the *levada*

runs underground for a short stretch. Cross a track leading
up left to a house (**45min**), then rejoin the watercourse.

When you reach a HAMLET and crossing track (**49min**),
leave the *levada* path and turn right along the track, which
immediately crosses over the *levada*. The track now
traverses more open, cultivated countryside, while the
watercourse, initially up to the left, crosses overhead four
minutes later (❹; **53min**), running towards Silves. Keep
left at a junction (**58min**), to pass the VILA MOSQUITO on
the left. At the Y-fork that follows, be sure to *go left* (the
right hand-fork passes a house with unfriendly dogs).
Then keep straight ahead on a track/then road and ascend
through the hamlet of **Vale da Lama** (**1h13min**), from
where there are fine views over the surrounding countryside. Descend to another road (**1h18min**) and turn left,
to pass the small PUMPING STATION (❶) on the right.

This was the 16min-point in the walk: cross the small
bridge over the *levada* and turn right, back to the MIRA-RIO
CAR PARK (❍; **1h34in**).

Walk 11: SILVES CIRCUIT

See also photograph page 20

Distance: 8.2km/5.1mi; 1h57min *(allow about 2h30min)*

Grade: ● easy. Little climbing is involved, and the tracks and paths used are mostly good underfoot.

Equipment: See pages 41-42.

Picnic suggestion: the windmill shown below (40min on foot; follow the main walk from the start; *no shade*)

How to get there and return: 🚌 from Portimão or Albufeira to Silves (Timetables 4, 5). Journey time 35-42min. 🚃 by train to Silves station (Timetable 9); the station lies some 2km/1.25mi south of Silves, and while there are bus connections into the town, they are infrequent. 🚗 by car: Park by the ring road, in the large parking areas provided on the south side of Silves (37° 11.091'N, 8° 26.501'W).

Short walk: Silves — windmill — Silves (4.8km/3mi; 1h05min).
● Easy. Follow the main walk for 32 minutes; return the same way.

Silves is a lovely old town situated on the River Arade. Apart from enjoying the ambience of the town square, there are several places of particular interest — including the castle, the cathedral, the museum and the old port area. Legend has it that Silves (or Cylpes, Chelb or Cilves, to use earlier names), was founded on its present site by the Cynetes some one thousand years BC, and since that time it has been occupied by a succession of races from all over Europe and Africa — including the Greeks and later the Romans, around the first century AD. Its subsequent history is turbulent, with bloody battles, times of peace and prosperity, total decline, and devastation by earthquakes. The museum is worth a visit, to see the coins and ceramics and other relics of these past civilisations and events. It is uphill to the right of the tower of the main gateway, in the old Moorish city walls, off the main square.

If you park in the car park, come by bus (it stops near the car park, by the tourist office) or arrive by train, follow

Windmill above Silves (Picnic 9)

signs for 'Câmara' (Town Hall), to direct you up to the main square. **Start the walk at the MAIN SQUARE (O) in Silves**: walk through the high arched gateway of the TOWER and head uphill, passing to the left of the CATHEDRAL (Sé; **4min**). The walk continues to the right at the junction just past the cathedral. (But first cross the junction and then go right to visit the castle, before returning to this point to continue; it is open daily except holidays from 09.00-19.00 in summer, but closes a little earlier in winter.) At the next junction, a minute later, keep left downhill, and stay beneath the walls of the CASTLE on the left. Coming to a crossroads (**11min**), turn left and then immediately fork right, on a track which leads between a fenced-off orange grove and large car park. Looking back, there are some especially fine views of Silves castle to be enjoyed.

As you approach a smallholding (**18min**), the track becomes concreted and continues up to the WATERCOURSE followed in Walk 10. Cross the narrow concrete footbridge and turn right on the path alongside the *levada* (❶). After just 60m/yds, take a path uphill to the left, towards a group of houses. As you reach them, less than two minutes later, turn left on the narrow surfaced

I T WAS THE ARABS who left behind the most impressive remains to be seen in Silves — the castle, the Albarranian Towers, the Almadinna walls, and the underground well. The castle enjoyed its heyday under the Moors in the 10th-12th centuries. During that period Silves was an important city, more important even than Lisbon. Situated in a rich agricultural region, it boasted opulent buildings, a thriving port, and markets.

The decline began in 1189, when Silves came under siege as part of the third crusade to oust the infidels from Algarve and spread Christianity. The slow decline of the city was finally completed by the earthquake of 1755, when the castle, the tower, and the town hall were badly damaged, and Silves ceased to be the capital of Algarve. Many of the walls are still intact, as is the underground well — romantically named 'Cisterna da Moura Encantada' (the enchanted Moorish girl's well).

You can enjoy all this at your leisure. If you look northeast as you walk the castle walls, you can see the old windmill shown opposite, perched on a hilltop. This lies on our route and is the destination of the Short walk. The cathedral, which you pass on the way to the castle, was built in Gothic style by King Afonso X during the last part of the 13th century. It became the cathedral of Algarve until, in the middle of the 16th century, the seat of the bishop was removed to Faro. Little is known about the fate of the silver treasures or the large library which were believed to have existed.

road; soon, at the next road junction, turn sharp right. Now you are heading towards the windmill, which is clearly in sight. The road continues around to the right, heading momentarily back towards Silves and the towering arches of the aqueduct. At the junction of roads by the AQUEDUCT (❷; **28min**), turn sharp left. Keep right at the fork encountered almost immediately. Turn right off the main road onto a lesser road (**35min**), to keep the windmill now up to the left. About a minute up the road, turn left on a track which dips towards the windmill then sweeps right towards a house. Pass the front of the house, then go left, straight up to the WINDMILL (❸; *P*9; **39min**). Despite the lack of shade, this is a very pleasant picnic spot, with a superb panorama over rolling *matos*-covered hills, with cultivated valleys and an excellent view of Silves. Portimão is visible on the seaward side, and the hills of the Serra de Monchique to the north. Close at hand, sticky-leaved cistus, *Cistus ladanifer*, and lavender, *Lavandula stoechas,* dominate in the dense vegetation; the green-winged orchid, *Orchis morio*, also finds a foothold.

Leave the windmill to continue along the undulating ridge, with your back to the sea. Follow the path along the ridge, keeping to the central spine. Good views open up now towards the Bastos Valley ahead on the right. Follow the path to the end of the ridge (**48min**), then turn left downhill, alongside a fenced enclosure. You pass a farmhouse on the left. At the end of the descent, turn right on a rising track, to meet a T-junction (**52min**). Go left, then keep round to the right at the top of the rise. Turn right almost immediately, along a track which at first keeps above the wooded valley down to the left. It then descends to a six-way junction (❹; **1h**), where you turn *sharp* left (the first track on the left) to continue downhill. Keep on this main track, which heads south beside a stream bed. Masses of lavender, olives and carobs now join the eucalyptus as you wind down through the valley. On joining a wide stabilised track (**1h17min**), turn left.

This track leads away from the *matos*-covered hills and back through cultivation towards Silves. The track becomes surfaced road (**1h24min**) as you approach the outskirts of the town, where you keep to the right-hand road on meeting housing. Just 150m/yds further on (almost immediately past a road on the left), turn left into a narrow WALKWAY (❺) at the side of a large ugly sub-station (**1h26min**) and climb steps which curve around to the right. A surfaced road is met a minute later. Turn left

Fábrica do Inglês — a cultural centre in Silves, incorporating the cork museum

9

and, in 90m/yds, take a track up right to the *levada*. Cross the FILTRATION POINT* (**6**) and turn left. Follow the path alongside the watercourse, which is now on your left. Cross a surfaced road (**1h38min**; there is a restaurant just 10 minutes downhill to the right here, closed 15.30-18.30 and all day Wednesdays) and continue alongside the *levada*.

The circuit is complete when you reach the concrete FOOTBRIDGE (**2**; **1h 42min**) crossed earlier in the walk; here turn down the track on the right to retrace your steps back to the MAIN SQUARE (**O**) in **Silves** (**1h57min**).

*There are warning signs on the gate at the filtration point, and care *is* needed here, especially if you have children with you. Try the gate knob, but if you find it locked, walk back to the road. Turn right and walk along the road for 0.5km. Then turn right on a narrow road. This leads back over the levada, where you can turn left to continue along the maintenance footpath. (By the way, if you were to stay on the road over the levada, heading towards Silves, after only another 300m/yds you would come to a typical Portuguese restaurant called 'Recanto dos Mouros' off to the right (open 12.00-15.30, then 18.30 till late; closed Wed). From the restaurant you could just continue towards Silves and turn left at the T-junction, soon getting back to the 11min-point in the walk (it's just 1.5km/1mi) from the filtration point back to the 11min-point.)

Walk 12: BENAGIL • MARINHA • ALBANDEIRA • SENHORA DA ROCHA • BENAGIL

See also photograph on page 21

Distance: 11.5km/7mi; 2h40min *(allow a good 4h)*

Grade: ● moderate. There is a steep valley, difficult to cross, in the final section of the walk, but it is well waymarked (PR1)

Equipment: See pages 41-42.

Picnic suggestions: beaches of Marinha (26min-point in the walk) or Albandeira (48min-point); both accessible by car; *no shade on either*

How to get there and return: 🚌 (Timetable 10) or 🚗 to/from Benagil. Approach Benagil from the N125, 3km east of the Lagôa roundabout and opposite the International School. The road is signposted from the Lagôa approach only, but signs appear at later junctions along this 5km stretch. Park near the café/restaurant 'O Algar' at the top of the hill, before descending to Benagil bay (37° 5.329'N, 8° 25.598'W). *Note:* This walk is easily followed in reverse from Senhora da Rocha. Either take a taxi from Armação de Pêra or walk the 2.5km/1.6mi from Hotel Garbe in Armação, initially towards Porches, then turn left opposite the petrol station.

Short walks (● both are easy)

1 Benagil — Praia da Marinha — Benagil (4.8km/3mi; 1h). Follow the main walk to the beautiful beach at Marinha. Return the same way.

2 Benagil — Praia da Albandeira — Benagil (8.0km/5mi; 1h40min). Follow the main walk to Praia da Albandeira, a small inlet, where there are café facilities in season. Return the same way.

This is another very picturesque section of the coast which is full of interest — from wild flowers to spectacular beaches. In our view, the beach at Marinha rates as one of the loveliest in Algarve and will probably stay so as long as it remains remote and difficult to get to. It lies in a beautiful natural setting and has the benefit of a small café/bar which is open only in season. The coastline along this section is extremely photogenic (see page 21 and overleaf), so be sure to carry your camera.

Benagil, where the walk starts, is a small fishing village where, if you wander down to the seafront, you will see the colourful fishing boats which are so typically Algarvian. Fish is still an important part of the diet in Portugal,

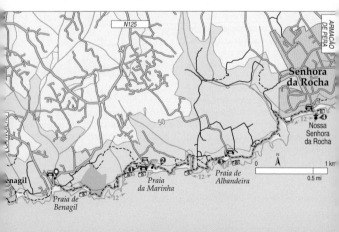

and it figures prominently on the menu in cafés and restaurants. Sardines *(sardinhas)* are a speciality of the area and, freshly caught and grilled (photograph page 13), they bear no relationship to the more familiar tinned product. They are at their best in the summer season and, traditionally, they are served with boiled potatoes. The finest accompaniment is a chilled bottle of *vinho verde*. The other national fish dish, which is even more popular, is *bacalhau*, dried salted cod. Cod used to be caught by Portuguese fishermen along the Grand Banks off Newfoundland, but now it mainly comes from Norway. The catch is salted, sun-dried and sold as flat, cardboard-like pieces which you'll see and smell in the supermarkets and markets all over Portugal. *Bacalhau*, pronounced 'backle-yow', is desalted and reconstituted by soaking in water and then can be cooked by any one of many hundreds of recipes. In a restaurant which caters primarily for locals there may be several *bacalhau* dishes on offer. Well-prepared and cooked in a tasty sauce, it is really delicious … but if you try it when it is not at its best, then the chances are that it will be your last try!

Start the walk from the RESTAURANT O ALGAR (**O**) at the top of the hill at **Benagil**: from the restaurant car park, take steps at the left of the building to a footpath. Keep left at a fork after 50m, then go right at the next fork, quickly coming to some fencing. From here to Praia da Marinha the walk is waymarked with the red and yellow flashes of the PR1, and there are several INFORMATION BOARDS in English. A fenced-off BLOW-HOLE is passed almost at once — the first of several en route. There is a wealth of wild flowers along this stretch in spring, including the tassel hyacinth, *Muscari comosum*, the woodcock orchid, *Ophrys scolopax* (which is not so common elsewhere in the region), the yellow bee orchid, *Ophrys lutea*, and many of the species already mentioned on page 52. Coastline erosion provides some interesting bays and weird formations too, which become especially photogenic later in the walk.

In **14min** the path starts to lead inland, to cross an inlet. First there is a diagonal descent to the left, before you go down right to cross the inlet and scramble up the far side, where you find the continuation of the coastal path (**20min**). Now you are at a wonderfully scenic part of the coast, and the views along the cliff, taking in all the incredible rock formations, are quite fantastic. Ahead is the CAR PARK for Marinha (**❶**; with picnic tables; **26min**).

Cross the car park to descend the steps in the far corner and continue along the surfaced path which is stepped in places. If you are stopping for a swim or just for photographs or refreshments, turn right down the steps three minutes later, to the superb sandy beach — **Praia da Marinha** (*P*12), a first suggestion for a beach picnic. Otherwise continue along the path which leads back to the cliff top and continues as the coastal path, passing another large fenced BLOW-HOLE (❷; **32min**), which you skirt on the seaward side. Coastal views along this walk include some tantalising sandy beaches which seem only to be accessible by boat. The one seen from here is shown on page 21. An inlet is encountered shortly (**36min**): walk down diagonally left to cross it and, as you rise into a clearing five minutes later, take the rough track which leads you back to the cliff edge. The rugged coastline, layered in strata of gold and cream, and sculptured into intriguing shapes by the restless energy of the sea, presents endless patterns. Another, shallow inlet is reached in **44min**. Here the naked man orchid, *Orchis italica*, finds a home amongst the rich flora. Then you come to the larger inlet of **Praia da Albandeira** (❸; *P*12; **48min**), another good setting for a picnic on the beach.

Continue behind the café/bar: cross the footbridge

behind the café and continue along the coastal path. There are views ahead of Armação de Pêra, which looks like villa-land from this distance (but you will turn back before it is reached). At **55min** a deep inlet requires an inland detour; then head back to the coast, and watch out for more blow-holes. In **1h02min** a very deep inlet is encountered: this one is only negotiable by footpaths which are difficult in places. Set off inland, staying at a high level, and ignore the first strong path descending to the right. Go down, diagonally right, following the *second* strong path (waymarked with YELLOW PAINT splodges). This is a steep and awkward descent towards the back of the beach. Reach the bottom in **1h09min** and turn left towards the back of the inlet, to find a path which goes uphill to a track on the far side of the inlet. Waymarked turns — right, left, right — lead you to a path which continues above this track, back in the direction of the sea. The superb beach at **Senhora da Rocha** is fully in view from a small headland (**1h15min**), and you pass the steps leading to the beach two minutes later.

Continue past the steps, if you want to visit the Roman-esque chapel of **Nossa Senhora da Rocha** (❹) on the headland (turn right at the junction reached in **1h19min**). Some cafés and restaurants lie to the left of this junction,

and Armação de Pêra is 2km further east. But our walk ends at this junction, and we retrace our steps to the restaurant O ALGAR above the beach at **Benagil** (**O**; **2h40min**).

The simple white church of Nossa Senhora da Rocha (Our Lady of the Rock) sits on a bluff dividing two coves. Although it was built in the 17th century, the two Visigothic columns used in its construction suggest that an earlier temple may well have existed on this site. Weekends see the local fishermen making their way to this headland. Taking up positions on the very edge, they are able to cast their lines out to sea.

Walk 13: CERRO • CONQUEIROS • PICO ALTO CIRCUIT

Distance: 10km/6.2mi; 2h25min *(allow about 4h)*

Grade: ● moderate. The trig point on Pico Alto stands at an elevation of 276m/905ft; Cerro itself lies on almost the same contour. There are two uphill sections: the climb up to the trig point is short and steep, while the later climb is more gradual. ***Important note:*** The main walk route outlined below is the most interesting, but can be overgrown. We carry secateurs to cut back rogue brambles and smile cheerily at the local who always pops up to tell us the route is no longer viable. Here are two alternative starts, if you don't want to get scratched. 1) Stay ahead two minutes along. At the T-junction, turn left downhill. You rejoin the main walk in 7min, at the 17min-point in the main walk. 2) Head along the ridge road towards Pico Alto. In around 10min, just after passing an old well and water tank down right and *before* a track forking left, turn right on a gravel track, towards a house (in Cumeada). As the track ends, follow a path to the right, pass a ruin on the left, and join a path forking left downhill (**❶**; the 12min-point in the main walk).

Equipment: See pages 41-42.

How to get there and return: 🚗 only accessible by car. Cerro lies 3.6km northwest of Alte. Approaching on the N124, turn north into Alte from the roundabout, then turn left almost immediately for 'Santa Margarida'. Turn left again in the centre of Santa Margarida for 'Serro' [sic]. Park 1.8km further on, beyond the dip with a high white wall on the left (37° 15.397'N, 8° 12.381'W). The walk starts on the road to the right, in the dip, signposted 'Conqueiros'.

Short walks (both ●)

1   **Cerro — Pico Alto boundary — Cerro** (5.6km/3.5mi; 1h16min; easy-moderate). Follow the main walk to the 12min-point and keep ahead along the trail. After 100m, in front of the houses of Cumeada, turn left on a track, to the ridge road. Turn right and follow the road for 1.2km, then, at the sign for the boundary of Pico Alto, go left on a track, picking up the main walk at (**❺**), to walk back to Cerro.

2   **Cerro — Pico Alto village — Cerro** (7.6km/4.7mi; 1h48min; easy). Follow Short walk 1, but keep ahead into Pico Alto village, where the road goes left. Then use the map to reach the trig point on Pico Alto. The path leaves from between the first and second houses on the right. Return the same way.

Cerro, Conqueiros and Pico Alto, like the villages of Alte and Pena, lie in the Barrocal region of Algarve. The Barrocal is a lens-shaped area of limestone which stretches from Cape St Vincent in the west, reaching its widest around the centre of Algarve (about 20km/12.5mi wide), before tapering out somewhere near Tavira. The limestones are dolomites and marls which are seen as whitish rocks, often weathering to dull grey. These are best observed in the scrub-covered ridges which form crests running parallel with the coast, as here on Pico Alto or, better still, in Walk 19 (Rocha da Pena; photograph page 108). The rich red soil *(terra rossa)* in the valleys between the ridges is highly fertile, and it is these areas which form the garden of Algarve. Orchards abound, and the crops include orange, fig, almond and carob. The almonds are

View north (inland) from the summit of Pico Alto, to Messines and the hills of the Serra de Monchique.

at their most spectacular in January and February when their delicate white and pale pink flowers are sprinkled randomly across the valleys and it is easy to see why they are sometimes called 'Algarvian snow.'

The plants give a good clue to the various distinct geological regions of Algarve, and the Barrocal provides the richest and most interesting flora. Many flowers typical of the region are seen on this walk, including wild jasmine, *Jasminum fruticans*, orchids, and the striking *Scilla peruviana*. Even the scrub (*matos*) is characteristic; there are more details of this in Walk 19. This walk leads through some timeless hamlets and a landscape created by generations of farmers living off the land.

Start the walk in the dip with the TALL WHITE WALL: head down the road signposted 'CONQUEIROS' (**O**). Pass a WASHHOUSE on the left and, in less than two minutes (after 150m/ys), turn left on a track with a WATER STORAGE AREA on the left corner. Wind through the old hamlet of **Cerro** and, as the track ends, go diagonally right and then left, to continue in the same direction. In spring, weeds may obscure the start of the path, but it soon becomes clear that you are on an old trail (secateurs could help at the start, see 'Grade', opposite). Where vegetation blocks the trail, continue alongside, down to the right.

The hamlet of Conqueiros soon comes into view ahead on the valley floor. In **12min**, at a JUNCTION (**❶**) where the return route comes in from the left, turn sharp right down a path, into the valley below. The path soon becomes a rough field track, before meeting the CERRO/CON-

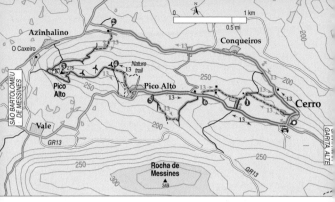

QUEIROS ROAD (opposite a small farmhouse; **17min**). Turn left down this road (right leads to back to Cerro). A peaceful rural ambience pervades this valley planted with olives, carobs and oranges; the heady scent of orange blossom filling the air in season. Just before reaching the hamlet, note the old WELL down to the right, on the far side of a wall (**25min**). Then rise up to walk through **Conqueiros (28min)**.

Now continue ahead on the road for almost 2km, ignoring roads and tracks right and left. The giant reed, *Arundo donax,* marks a stream bed down to the left. Then watch for a HIGH CORK OAK arching almost all the way across the road and painted (at time of writing) with the number '4'. About 25m past the tree, just before a CULVERT (❷), fork left on a clear path, to cross a small stream bed (**48min**). The path rises, passes to the left of a farm building, and meets a crossing lane. Cross over and keep ahead on a field track, which reverts to path. Stay with the track/path as it skirts to the left of a citrus grove and then a field, heading towards the Pico Alto ridge. The path gradually heads towards a fence with concrete posts, over to the right. Cross the overflow stream coming from a WATER TANK on the right (**53min**). Less than a minute later, the path heads across the top end of the fence and continues between a terrace on the right and a bank on the left. After dipping across an eroded channel, the path rises through a patch of cistus. When you meet a diagonally crossing two-wheel track (**57min**), follow it to the left in a zigzag, rising to a T-junction with another crossing track (**1h**). Turn right on this track, to continue contouring along the ridge with wide-reaching views.

At a junction of tracks (**1h08min**), when the motorway viaduct comes into view ahead, turn left uphill. (But you could turn right downhill here, then right again on a lane down to the main road, after seven minutes coming to an excellent restaurant just to the right (closed Tuesdays).

Get into low gear for a short steep climb to the SUMMIT of **Pico Alto** (❸; **1h20min**). This is the spot for a picnic, with fantastic views over much of the surrounding countryside. And around your feet there are yet more orchids, one of particular interest being the mirror orchid — or rather a special form of it, in which the lip of the flower has become elongated to resemble an insect. It is *Ophrys speculum ssp lusitanica.*

To continue, return to where the uphill track came in from the right. Take the track to the left here, heading past two WIND TURBINES on the ridge. At the THIRD TURBINE, take the path just past a carob tree on the left, opposite a NO 1 MARKER POST (❹; **1h31min**). Follow this to a junction of paths (**1h34min**) and turn right through a gap in a wall. A few strong paths now head towards Pico Alto village, including a NATURE TRAIL, but you want to go across the middle of the ridge, *towards telegraph wires* and the village rooftops which are soon in view.

Soon you enter a walled-in trail. You come into the centre of **Pico Alto** VILLAGE less than five minutes later, emerging between two houses. Turn left here, to reach the road on a bend (**1h39min**). *(Short walk 2 comes in on this bend.)* Follow this ridge road for about 150m; then, at a sign ('POMAR'; ❺) signalling the exit from Pico Alto , turn right on a track. After 150m fork left on a path and follow this for about 400m to a T-junction with a track, with a WATER TANK down right. Turn left uphill. Stay on this track, which rises at first, then levels out and passes behind a building on the right. Keep ahead into a walled track which swings left to reach the ROAD (**1h59min**).

Turn right, past a house, for 150m; then, at the back of the sign denoting the Loulé boundary, turn left and then almost immediately right on a path. After another 150m this approaches the old farm of Cumeada, where the trail is too overgrown to follow. Go left to wind through the complex, then walk under a huge carob tree (**2h03min**) and head diagonally right uphill. When you rejoin the path from the old farm, turn left. Two minutes later, at a white building, go right and then left, to pass the front of this row of renovated houses (**Cumeada**). The trail becomes a track at this point, and soon swings right, back towards the road: keep ahead along another trail here. Just past a ruin on the left you're back at the 12min-point in your outward route (❶; **2h10min**). Retrace your steps back to the PARKING PLACE (◯; **2h25min**).

Walk 14: ALTE • SOIDOS • ALTE

See also photograph on page 45

Distance: 8.7km/5.4mi; 2h20min *(allow about 3h30min)*

Grade: ● moderate. The outward route leads steadily uphill, often through old olive terraces. The final climb to the trig point of Rocha dos Soidos at 467m/1530ft is another steady (rather than steep) ascent. Some of the paths and tracks are stony underfoot.

Equipment: See pages 41-42.

Picnic suggestion: Fonte Grande (no walking; park at the picnic site)

How to get there and return: 🚗 only accessible by car; park at Fonte Grande (37° 14.328'N, 8° 10.136'W).

Shorter walk: Alte circuit (6.7km/4.2mi). ● Moderate. Do the main walk, but miss out the diversion to the trig point: turn right at the 53min-point (❹) and pick up the notes again at the 1h27min-point.

Short walk: Fonte Grande circuit (2.5km/1.6mi; 45min). ● Easy. Ignore the start of the main walk and continue ahead past Fonte Grande, with the river on the right. Stay ahead when the road reverts to track, passing a café on the right. In around 12min, immediately after a stone wall topped with concrete posts on the left, turn left on a field track. Soon, stay right on an old walled-in trail/path as the track forks left (the trail *does* continue ahead despite some invasive vegetation). As the walled-in section ends, ignore a strong path through the wall to the left. Your path veers a little to the right and meets a crossing path. Turn left here, then soon fork left, above the valley down to the left. In four minutes step right through a low stone wall and continue in the same direction. Stay left at cross-paths, then drop left down the terrace wall and descend gradually along the hillside back to the start of the walk.

Alternative start from Alte. Park as suggested in Car tour 3, page 27 (37° 14.006'N, 8° 10.751'W). Take the road to the right of the church towards the Fontes but soon, by a *farmacia* (chemist) on the left, follow Rua da Serra uphill to the tarmac road above Alte. Go right (ahead) for 3min, to a hairpin bend, then keep ahead on a track (18min) which bends right and becomes a rough stony path. Stay ahead to join a red/yellow locally waymarked path coming up from the right. Continue along the main walk, using notes from (❶).

A large part of the walk we originally devised to visit the Rocha dos Soidos trig point has now been enclosed as a private hunting area and is no longer accessible. Fortunately the trig point itself lies just outside the fenced area and can still be reached. This new route is a

little more challenging in that it uses fairly steadily rising footpaths and tracks, some waymarked, to the summit. The return route starts out the same way, but diverges at Soidos de Baixo to connect with our original route back to Fonte Grande. *Only follow waymarks that are mentioned in the text!*

Start the walk just west of **Fonte Grande**: opposite a gated house, take a path rising to the north (**O**). Red/yellow waymarks soon appear. In a few minutes you reach a path junction where the 'Alternative start' joins from the left (**❶**). Turn right here; follow the waymarks, initially staying above Fonte Grande, then heading left uphill. The path becomes a two-wheeled field track which emerges on a road (**23min**). Take the left fork opposite, into **Soidos de Baixo** (**❷**). At a junction almost immediately, with a FOUNTAIN/TAP ahead on the right, turn left uphill on concrete road. In a few minutes (after just over 400m), on a bend to the left, turn right on a track.

Apart from the waterfalls just below Alte, its main attraction is this spring, Fonte Pequena, and another spring half a kilometre further along the river — Fonte Grande, with a well-equipped picnic site, café, bar/restaurant and car parking (Car tour 3).

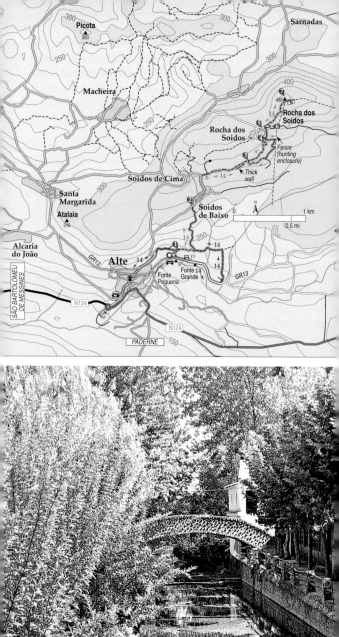

Stay ahead past a track right to a threshing floor. In just over two minutes, when the track swings left, stay ahead on a contouring path (which becomes a rough track/path). Just after passing a very THICK STONE WALL on the right, note the path joining from the right (**3**; **41min**); it is the return route. Around four minutes later, follow the waymarks left uphill and wind up to a wide terrace, where you turn right. At the end of a level section of terrace, follow the waymarks left uphill onto another wide terrace. Continue to the left, then fork right uphill for a short scramble onto a higher terrace. Initially go left, then briefly right uphill. Go right now and straight ahead along the path. In under two minutes, the path heads left, up to a track (**4**; **53min**).

To the right is the return route, but turn left into the hamlet of **Rocha dos Soidos** (**5**). You reach a walled-in track. Note the white summer house across the field ahead to the right as you turn left to meet the concrete village road. Very soon, as the wall on the right ends, turn right on a clear red earthen path (still waymarked). This leads behind the WHITE SUMMER HOUSE (**6**) and over a wall (another wall is to the left) and straight up to the **Rocha dos Soidos** SUMMIT (**7**; **1h10min**).

Return the same way to the 53min-point (**4**; **1h 27min**), but stay ahead down the two-wheeled track. You pass close to the FENCED HUNTING AREA on the left before the fence angles away to the left. Soon, at a fork, keep right. The track peters out into a path and rises gently. Swing slightly right uphill and, at another fork, stay right. You rise back to the 41min-point of your outward track (**3**). Turn left and retrace your steps back to **Soidos de Baixo** (**2**) and from there back down to **Fonte Grande** (**0**; **2h20min**).

Walk 15: PADERNE • CASTELO • AZENHAL • PADERNE

Distance: 13.5km/8.4mi; 3h *(allow 4-5h)*

Grade: ● easy-moderate. Some paths, but the walk is mainly on tracks — sometimes stony, but mostly good underfoot; uphill sections are few.

Equipment: See pages 41-42.

Picnic suggestion: Paderne Castle (30min on foot, or drive there)

How to get there and return: 🚗 car or 🚌 bus from Albufeira to/from Paderne (Timetable 7). Journey time 21min. Travelling by car, park near the stadium and health centre (37° 10.549'N, 8° 12.232'W).

Short walks (● all of these varied and interesting versions are easy)

1   **Paderne — Castelo — Paderne** (6.9km/4.3mi; 1h20min). Follow the main walk as far as the castle and return to the motorway, then pick up the main walk again at the 2h23min-point.

2   **Paderne — Castelo — Albufeira road** (7.2km/4.5mi; 1h35min). Follow the main walk to the 1h32min-point, then turn left to the N395 road at Cerro do Ouro, for a bus to Albufeira.

3   **Paderne — old bridge — Paderne** (8.0km/5mi; 1h42min). Follow the main walk to the castle and on to the bridge (51min). Return from the bridge, following the main walk from the 2h08min-point.

4   **Paderne circuit** (9.4km/5.8mi; 1h45min). This walk includes the castle, bridge, and watermill. Follow the main walk to the 51min-point. Turn right (instead of left) just over the bridge, and follow the footpath along the river to the mill. Cross the weir to the far bank and follow the track back to the motorway bridge (see footnote on page 99). Return by picking up the main walk at the 2h23min-point.

Alternative walk: See page 99 (with map section enlargement).

Paderne Castle dates back to the times of the Moors. Built on a hill and surrounded on three sides by the River Quarteira, it had a role in the defence of the region during the period of Arab occupation.

Start the walk from **Paderne** STADIUM (**○**) on the BOLIQUEIME ROAD below the town. Head towards Purgatório, passing a CEMETERY on the left. Then ignore a first turn-off left (the return route) but take the *second* left, signed 'FONTE/CASTELO'. Follow this lane through cultivation, to pass a fountain (*fonte;* **14min**). Very soon, turn right on a track ('CASTELO'; **❶**). The castle now comes into view ahead, beyond orange and olive groves. Bear left on the main track, going under the MOTORWAY. Just after the motorway (**30min**), where the main track goes up left to the castle, keep ahead towards the river on a lesser track. Almost immediately take the diagonal path climbing steeply left up the hillside. In spring, look out for orchids now, including the lovely *Ophrys bombyliflora* (bumblebee orchid).

You reach **Paderne Castle** (**❷**; *P*13) in **37min**. It's a good picnic spot: from one side of the castle there are open views towards Paderne; the other side looks down on the fascinating arched bridge which was part of an old route.

We go there next. Facing the front of the castle, leave by a small path along the left side of the castle; at first you are looking down over the old bridge. The path does not descend immediately, but contours up-river and away from the bridge. After three minutes, the path goes left and descends to the river. You meet a strong crossing path by the riverside (**43min**). *(A right here returns to the 30min point.)* Follow the path downstream towards the bridge, with the river on the right. *Arundo donax*, the giant reed, grows tall by the river, while the dwarf fan palm, *Chamaerops humilis*, is at home in the arid ground on the other side of the path.

The BRIDGE (❸) is reached in **51min**. Cross it and turn left. *(The return route enters from the right here, and this is where Short walk 4 turns right.)* At first continue along the river but, in just over a minute, take the strong path uphill to the right — a steady climb. Near the top, the path veers right towards a ruin. Before reaching the ruin, turn left on a rising path which meets a faint field track

Paderne Castle (Picnic 13), from the bridge over the Quarteira River

Paderne Castle was conquered in 1249, during the reign of Don Afonso III, but history does not record whether the battle was fierce and bloody or whether the castle was damaged. In 1305 it was given by Don Dinis to the Master of the Order of Aviz, Don Lourenço Annes, suggesting that the castle was still in use in that period. Today only the outer walls remain sufficiently intact to remind us of its past grandeur. Much of the interior has been destroyed, although there are still some remains of the chapel dedicated to Our Lady of the Ascension. The nearby high-arched bridge spanning the river is believed to date from an earlier period, from Roman times, when the river was navigable. It was rebuilt sometime in the Middle Ages, probably by the Crusaders, and it has survived the ravages of time remarkably well.

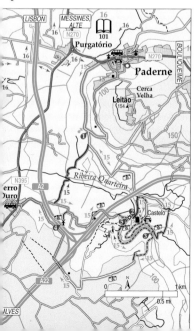

coming from the ruin. Turn left on this track, back across the top of the valley you just climbed. The track becomes more distinct as it bends to the right. Much of the climbing is over in **1h06min** and, as you start to descend a little, there are wider views to enjoy through the almond groves.

Turn left when you reach a T-junction (**1h12min**; *the Alternative walk goes right here*). Two minutes later, turn right at another T-junction. Head for the bridge over the motorway. Once over the MOTORWAY BRIDGE, continue ahead. Follow the narrow country road as it swings away to the right (**1h20min**), with the motorway not far away over to the right. At a T-junction (**1h32min**), go right. (*A left turn here leads to the Albufeira/Paderne road at Cerro do Ouro in five minutes; Short walk 2.*) Immediately, the road passes beneath the motorway and heads back towards the river. *A short-cut back to Paderne is passed three minutes later (**1h35min**)**. A few minutes later, turn right up a track to an old WINDMILL (**❹**; **1h45min**). The machinery is still in place, but take care if you venture inside — it looks in danger of collapsing. Fine views are on offer, with the hills to the north drawing the eye.

Return to the road and turn right. The castle comes into view ahead (**1h52min**) as you reach a crossroads after about 450m. Follow the road to the left here, skirting a white farmhouse on the right. Cross the MOTORWAY BRIDGE, and stay left (**1h56min**). As the castle comes into view again, you pass beneath a SIGN, 'AZENHA', and the road reverts to track. Very soon (**1h59min**), take a path down to the right; it cuts a bend off the track and descends to an OLD MILL (AZENHA!; **❺**; **2h01min**). (The track sweeps down to the river just *beyond* this mill, where *Short walk 4 and the Alternative walk both rejoin the main walk.*)

Turn right to continue past the mill** on a riverside path, beside paper-white *Narcissus papyraceus* (photograph

*You could save 2.5km/40min here by following part of PR1. At the top of the rise, where Quinta do Loureiro and a PR1 sign are on the right (1h35min), turn left, to join a narrow walled track. Descend to a T-junction and turn left, then right, to the river. Use the tall concrete blocks to cross the river to a wall, and continue along a narrow ledge (with handrail) to a track on the far bank. (It's possible to paddle when the river is low, but it could be slippery; in summer it's usually dry.) Continue along the track, but after about 550m, *turn left* opposite another PR1 sign on the right. This track emerges on the main *castelo* track (1h55min). Turn left to pass an old *quinta* on the left and in under two minutes reach the 2h38min-point of the main walk.

**If the river is low here, the walk can be shortened by crossing the WEIR and retracing the outward route from the 30min-point. But note that in places the weir can be very slippery when wet.

page 123) and colonies of the Spanish bluebell, *Endymion hispanicus*. Cross the BRIDGE (❸; **2h08min**) and turn right on a track *(Short walk 3 rejoins here.)* (Or turn left and follow the path by the river back to the 30min-point.) Climb to a cross-track (**2h13min**) and turn left. Stay with the main track as you crest the small hill and start to descend. When you join the track to the castle (**2h18min**), keep right downhill. Ignore the track joining from the right four minutes later.

On reaching your outward route (**2h23min**), turn right under the MOTORWAY. *(Short walk 1 rejoins here.)* Back at the T-junction near the *fonte* on the left (❷; **2h38min**), turn right. In three minutes, take a rough track up left, which becomes surfaced by a house on the left. When you come to some apartments (**2h54min**), keep around to the right. Pass a SCHOOL on the left, descend to the CEMETERY, and turn right to the STADIUM in **Paderne** (❶; **3h**).

Alternative walk: Paderne — Azenhal — Paderne (11.5km/7.1mi; 2h34min; ● grade as main walk). Follow the main walk to the 1h12min-point (❹), then keep right, downhill, on the track. After three minutes (ⓑ; 1h15min), follow the main track off right, towards the castle. It passes a ruined farm, becoming a field track along the ridgetop as it heads north-east. Follow it round to the left, beneath electricity cables and to the left of a pylon. As the track forks (ⓒ), keep ahead on a path towards the motorway and a white farmhouse. The faint path leads down into a field. Head across the field for only 25 paces, keeping to the right, and then turn right through a gap in the foliage. Beyond the gap go diagonally left;  then, almost at once, swing back left towards the white farmhouse. A wall on your left and another wall ahead funnel you into an old path descending into the valley. On meeting an old trail in the bottom, turn right. Keep right at the fork a minute later and right again at the next fork. You emerge on the river bank (1h30min). To the left is Azenhal; to the right is your continuation: pick up the main walk at the 2h01min-point (❻).

(ⓑ) *Option 1:* Fork left off the main track here, onto a lesser track. In the dip below the motorway, go right on a path, with an overgrown old trail on the left. In a further 3min, go left, then right to join the old trail. Follow the rising trail into the motorway access road, to soon reach the 1h56min-point in the main walk (1h30min). Now refer again to the map for the main walk: either go right downhill with the main walk, or turn left and reverse the main walk for 15min, back to the 1h35min-point, then cross the motorway bridge and omit the windmill diversion.

(ⓒ) *Option 2, very steep:* Go right at the fork, following the track into a field. Keep to the left of the field, and go left through the gap at the bottom of the field. Head right to the next pylon (fine views). *Carefully* descend the steep path from here to the river, emerging close by Azenhal.

See photograph page 9

Distance: 11.2km/7mi; 2h48min *(allow about 4h)*

Grade: ● moderate. Three short uphill sections and a total height gain of under 250m/820ft; the tracks and paths are mainly good underfoot. The ford across the river is usually dry outside the winter months: check its level and flow when you cross the bridge on leaving Paderne to decide whether or not to shorten the second section of the walk. Take care along the short road-walking sections. Yellow/red waymarked PR2

Equipment: See pages 41-42.

How to get there and return: as for Walk 15, page 96. (There is also a large parking area at the start of the road to the castle.)

Short walks (both are ●)

1 **Cerro de São Vicente circuit** (7.3km/4.6mi; 1h49min). Follow the main walk as far as the 1h28min-point (when you return to ❶), then stay ahead under the motorway to retrace your outward route back to Paderne.

2 **Country circuit north of Paderne** (7km/4.4mi; 1h41min). Follow the start of the main walk as far as the 21min-point (❶) and turn right on the track beside the motorway. Now pick up the main walk notes at the 1h28min point and follow them to the end.

This pleasant walk through gently undulating country-side behind the coastal plain passes two windmills at the highest point on the hill called **Cerro de São Vicente** (168m/550ft) — one restored (but without sails), the other a ruin.

Start the walk at the STADIUM in **Paderne** (**O**) by heading back (west) towards Purgatorio, passing the CEME-TERY on the left. (The chapel of Nossa Senhora ao Pe da Cruz is on the opposite side of the road.) Follow the main road through **Purgatorio** (keep left at the Y-fork with the 'no entry' sign) and towards Albufeira for 1km then turn right into a narrow road signposted 'MATOS DE BAIXO' (**14min**). Go under the MOTORWAY and almost immediately note the track off to the right, alongside the motorway (❶; **21min**) — it's the continuation of the main walk or Short walk 2.

Go left into the *next* track. Turn right three minutes later on a farm track with a stone wall on the left. Soon, the track curls round left, but stay ahead now on a strong path (**28min**), which winds uphill. There are fine views inland to enjoy as the path steadily rises. On coming to a high stone wall on the right (**33min**), continue round to the right on a strong path; the sea is now over to your left. Still rising, you reach the highest point on **Cerro de São Vicente** (❷; **38min**). Take the track off right to have a closer look at the two windmills — one restored but sail-less, the other a ruin.

Then descend the track which becomes tarmac. Ignore

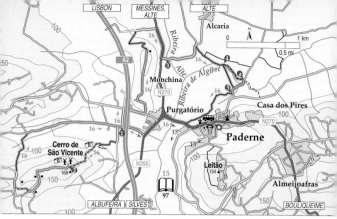

a track to the left and stay ahead on road, to pass between two white houses. As you approach a crossroads, the waymarks send you right — initially into the drive of the house uphill to the right and then on a path below the house (**54min**). Rejoining the road, rise to cross a SADDLE (the road reverts to track before reaching the top). At a fork, where the main track goes left; go right on a lesser track (**59min**). Descend to a tarmac road (**1h08min**) and turn right.

Return towards the motorway. Pass the track you took earlier, on your right and, a minute later, go left on the track beside the motorway (**❶**; the 21min-point on the outward route, now **1h28min**). *(But keep ahead here to return on Short walk 1.)* On meeting a road, turn right back underneath the motorway. Rise back towards Purgatorio but turn left on a road signposted to 'MONCHINA' (**1h36min**). Continue uphill, now on a rough tarmac road, which leads along a ridge before ending at a large house (**1h50min**) on the right. Now on track, reach a T-junction and turn right. Ignore tracks left and right; continue straight downhill to the main road (**2h 03min**). Turn right but, in six minutes turn left towards 'ALCARIA', immediately crossing a bridge over the **Ribeira Alte** (**❸**).

You are now on a quiet tarmac road. Just in front of the VILLAGE SIGN (**2h18min**), turn right on a pleasantly shady narrow cinder track. This leads to the **Ribeira de Álgibre** (**❹**; **2h24min**), which you cross heading diagonally left.*
After crossing, you come to a road that leads to Paderne (**2h30min**): turn right but soon (**❺**; before crossing a bridge), turn right on a meandering track, with Paderne over to the left. Coming to the main N125 (**2h44min**), turn left, back to the STADIUM in **Paderne** (**O**; **2h48min**).

*If the river is too high here, fork left and follow a narrow path to the road (**❹**) , then turn right and pick up the walk again at (**❺**).

Walk 17: RIBEIRA DE ALGIBRE CIRCUIT

Distance: 11km/6.9mi; 2h43min *(allow 3h30min-4h)*

Grade: ● easy-moderate. The outward leg of this track walk contours gently at low level, while the return section rises about 80m/265ft.

Equipment: See pages 41-42.

How to get there and return: 🚌 only accessible by car: Take the N270 Boliqueime to Loulé road. Soon after crossing over the A22 motorway at Junction 11 and passing a quarry on the left, turn left towards Parragil. At the T-junction in Parragil turn left again. Then keep ahead at crossroads (still in Parragil): from here it is 3.5km/2.2mi to Ribeira de Algibre; park where the houses end, just before the bridge (37° 11.134'N, 8° 5.108'W).

Short walk: Riverside walk at Ribeira de Algibre (2.5km/1.6mi; 36min). ● Easy, mainly level walking. Start by following the main walk to the T-junction reached in 18min. Turn right here (the main walk turns left) and follow the track back to the main road. A right turn now leads back to the starting point after just three minutes.

This walk explores a little know part of the Algarve's beautiful Barrocal. As always in this region you can expect to find a varied landscape of farmland, light woodland, rich vegetation and some interesting flowers — especially throughout the spring months, with plenty of wild orchids tucked away along the side of the track.

Start the walk in the HAMLET of **Ribeira de Algibre** (O): take the track on the east side of the main road (the right-hand side of the road, if you approached from Parragil). After a short while the track veers towards the **Ribeira de Algibre** and continues alongside it. Further along, stay with the track as it turns abruptly right, ignoring the vague track ahead leading towards a farm. You reach a T-JUNCTION (❶) with a major track in **18min**; on the return we will be following this track back to the start. *(For now, the Short walk turns right here.)*

Turn left and simply follow this long stretch of main track — where there are good orchids to be found in spring — ignoring all forks right and left, until you descend to a junction of tracks at FORD over the **Ribeira de Algibre** (❷; **1h06min**). There is, however, no river crossing for us on

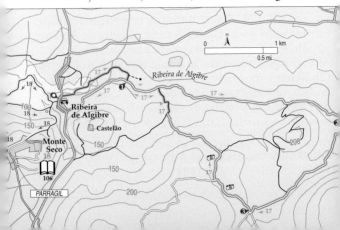

The ford over the Ribeira de Algibre, reached at about 1h06min

this circuit; instead, turn right and head uphill on the main track through yet more varied countryside. The climbing continues steadily for some time until it levels out a little before a strong track on the right is reached. Ignore this track and continue ahead to a MAJOR JUNCTION (❸; **1h37min**).

There is more climbing ahead after turning right at this junction and soon there are good views over the surrounding countryside as you reach the highest point in this walk at 207m/680ft. Another junction is reached (**1h56min**), as you start into gentle descent: turn right here. As you start to descend views towards Monte Seco with its tall mast open up. Stay on the main track as it bends left, ignoring the earthen track ahead. Keep on this main track, ignoring all other junctions, as it winds down to a T-junction with the outgoing route (**2h18min**). Turn left here and notice, around eight minutes later, the track on the right (❶) which was on your outward route. Keep ahead; your track acquires a tarmac surface before joining the main road. Turn right to head back to the car and the start of the walk at **Ribeira de Algibre** (❍; **2h43min**).

Walk 18: MONTE SECO CIRCUIT

Distance: 9.5km/6mi; 2h02min *(allow about 3h)*

Grade: ● moderate. There are two short sections of steep uphill walking and a stony descent to the riverside. The diversion to the trig point adds 0.8km/0.5mi and 10min to the main walk total.

Equipment: See pages 41-42.

How to get there and return: 🚗 only accessible by car: Take the N270 Boliqueime to Loulé road. Soon after crossing over the A22 motorway at Junction 11 and passing a quarry on the left, turn left towards Parragil. At the T-junction in Parragil turn left again. Then keep ahead at crossroads (still in Parragil): from here it is 3.5km/2.2mi to Ribeira de Algibre; park where the houses end, just before the bridge (37° 11.134'N, 8° 5.108'W).

Shorter walks

1 Ribeira de Algibre — Monte Seco hamlet — Ribeira de Algibre (7.5km/4.7mi; 1h38min). ● Moderate, with only one short section of uphill walking. Follow the main walk to the 27min-point (❸). Keep ahead now to continue along the contour of the hill, passing a white house below on the right. Ignore tracks left and right. In 32min, there is a fine well on the left, as the track describes a U round the head of a gully. Keep ahead, ignoring tracks forking right (at 34min and 40min). When you reach a T-junction (48min), turn right downhill, picking up the main walk at the 1h12min-point (❺).

2 Algibre Valley (8km/5mi; 1h40min). ● Easy, level track-walking. Start along the main walk and go right at the first junction (❶), then fork right in 15min. Keep along this track, ignoring side-tracks, as it meanders along the Ribeira de Algibre, never far from the river over to the right. In 36min you pass the point where the main walk enters from the left (❻; the 1h26min-point in the main walk). Continue to where you can easily get down to the river (about 50min — beyond the cultivated fields, where the track forks right). The walk can be as long or short as you like; just return the same way.

Poppy fields near the Ribeira de Algibre

3   Ribeira de Algibre — Monte Seco hamlet — Ribeira de Algibre
(3.2km/2mi; 40min). ● Easy. Follow the main walk to the 19min-point
(❷), then return down the track on the right. Ignore a track up to the
right, but turn right further on (28min). Ten minutes later, pass your
outgoing field track up to the right and continue left, to cross the diagonal
field track. Return to the walled-in track and follow it back to the start.

S et in the hills and valleys of the limestone Barrocal (see
Walk 13), this is a scenic country circuit in any season,
but especially interesting to wild flower lovers in spring.
Paeonia broteroi (photograph page 123) and poppies are
amongst the showy flowers on the lower sections, while
the seemingly-dry hillsides abound with wild orchids.

Start the walk in the HAMLET of **Ribeira de Algibre**
(**O**): turn left (west) along the track on the south (Parragil)
side of the BRIDGE. At the TRACK JUNCTION (**❶**) soon
reached, go diagonally left. *(Or right for Shorter walk 2.)*
Shortly, as the main track swings right, stay ahead up a
field track. An old THRESHING FLOOR is just to the right.
Now in a steady uphill climb, the track bends right to
eventually pass a track joining from the left (**9min**). Stay
ahead, uphill, to run into a concrete road five minutes later.
Keep ahead into an open area, and descend to the centre
of **Monte Seco** (**❷**; **19min**), where a left turn meets the
main road. *(The track to the right is the return route of Short
walk 3.)* Opposite is the local, authentic café/bar/shop and
to the right is the café/bar Bar do Monte; aside from the
café at Ribeira de Algibre, these are the only places for
refreshments on the walk.

Turn right here and right again less than a minute (after
50m) later, on a narrow road. When this road soon reverts
to track, keep ahead. There are extensive views over the
Algibre Valley as this high-level track undulates round the
hill. Just short of the top of a sharp rise, not far before a
white house below on the right, turn left uphill on a track
(**❸**; **27min**). *(Shorter walk 1 continues ahead here.)*

Stay on this track in a steady ascent towards the summit
of **Monte Seco**. Walled enclosures pattern the valley to the
right. Monte Seco's trig point, over to the left, is marked
by a mobile phone mast. The track soon swings away from
the trig point and descends to a T-junction (**44min**),
where the main walk turns right. From this position, the
trig point is easily seen back to the left. (To reach the TRIG
POINT on **Monte Seco** (**❹**; 296m/971ft), a panoramic
viewpoint, turn *left* here, towards a farmhouse. In two
minutes, turn left through a wide gap in a stone wall and
head diagonally across to the trig point — this takes five
minutes).

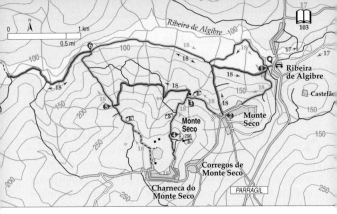

The track, soon concreted, descends between buildings to a narrow surfaced road (**50min**). Turn right uphill; the road bends right in under four minutes. At a junction (**55min**), go right on a rising concrete track, which leads to a house less than two minutes later. Stay ahead here up a walled-in trail, passing a circular THRESHING FLOOR on the right. Reach a T-junction (**1h**) and turn left. Deserted hamlets, almond and olive groves feature in the landscape along this very pleasant route. Do not be tempted to stray down right when the trail becomes a field track for a short distance; it soon reverts back to a walled-in trail.

When you reach a T-junction with a track (**1h05min**), turn right (north). As the track starts to descend, Monte Seco's trig point can be seen again, across the valley to the right. Where a track goes left (**1h09min**), keep straight downhill. Care is needed now, as the track becomes quite stony. Across the valley ahead lies Espargal, while a line of giant *Arundo donax* reeds in the valley floor marks the bed of the Algibre River. Shortly, you pass a track on the right (**⑤**; **1h12min**). *(Shorter walk 1 rejoins here.)* Nine minutes later, ignore a minor track to the right; continue downhill. The track swings right, almost parallel with the river below to the left, before heading left to the valley floor and a T-JUNCTION of tracks (**⑥**; **1h26min**). Turn right here *(left is the outward route of Shorter walk 2)*.

There is chance to relax now as the track meanders through delightful countryside, following the line of the **Ribeira de Algibre** on the left. When you reach a junction (**1h50min**) go left, following the river over to the left, back to the HAMLET of **Ribeira de Algibre** (**○**; **2h02min**).

Walk 19: PENINA CIRCUIT

See map opposite

Distance: 6.5km/4mi; 1h34min *(allow about 2h30min)*

Grade: ● moderate. Rocha da Pena peaks at 479m/1571ft and the starting point is 300m/984ft, so there is little climbing. Apart from a stretch of stony track on the descent to Penina, the paths and tracks are generally good. Jeep safaris, in high season, can make the track between Penina and the *fonte* very dusty. Red/yellow waymarked (PR18)

Equipment: See pages 41-42.

Picnic suggestion: Rocha da Pena (7min on foot; follow Walk 19)

How to get there and return: 🚗 only accessible by car. Travelling from Pena towards Salir on the N124, turn north at Taipa (1km short of Salir), following signs for Rocha da Pena and Alcaria. After passing through Alcaria, turn left towards Rocha da Pena. Keep ahead and park where the road ends at the Fonte dos Amoados in Rocha, or alongside the wide track just beyond it (37° 15.017'N, 8° 5.891'W). (*Note:* An environmental centre in Pena village is worth a stop. It is located on the N124 in the old school at the west end of the village. This walk can be easily started from Penina as well.)

Longer walk: Windmill circuit and trig point (9km/5.8mi; 2h20min). ● Moderate. Park as for the main walk. Follow the main walk as far as the trig point (❸; 52min). Then return to the circular clearing (❶) and pick up the notes for the *Alternative walk* from the 21min-point.

Alternative ascent via the windmills (8km/5mi; 1h44min). ● Moderate-difficult; a more challenging route for fit and agile walkers. Start from the *fonte* (**O**): walk along the road towards Pena, then fork left immediately on the diagonally rising track. In 14min cross a minor track (❺), to reach the windmills (❻; 16min). Return to the track crossing and turn right uphill. As the track levels out (19min), turn back sharp left uphill. In under a minute, just as the rough field track starts to descend, turn right uphill on a path. After a few minutes the main path, which rises ahead gradually, becomes faint and is easily missed. (Be aware of an unseen drop to the left into an old disused quarry.) You may find yourself on a more obvious route not far to the right of the original path: this becomes a scramble, at first rising gently, but then more steeply as you approach the top. Once on top, head left to a circular clearing (❶; 35min), and pick up the notes from the 21min-point in the main walk.

Alternative walk: Windmill circuit (4km/2.5mi; 1h08min). ● Moderate, but a tricky section down the hillside to the windmills, on a very faint, easily missed path; requires careful footwork. Park as for the main walk. Follow the main walk to the 21min-point (❶; the circular clearing). Continue ahead on the track beyond the clearing. After just a minute, take a path left to the 'Miradouro Norte' (❼) for a splendid view north to the Serra do Caldeirão. Then return to the track from the circular clearing and turn left. The track peters out into a path. *Take care* not to stray off the route to the right, as there is an unseen steep drop into an old disused quarry. Continue downhill, to emerge on a field track. Go left here, meet another track (35min) and turn right. You reach a stabilised track two minutes later (❺), where you turn left to the windmills (❻; 40min). Enjoy the fine views, then return along the stabilised track which gradually descends the hillside back to the *fonte* (**O**).

T his is another walk through the Barrocal limestones of Algarve (see Walk 13 for more details), but only on the diversion to the summit of Rocha da Pena do you

Seven minutes into the walk there is a very pleasant picnic spot close to the weathered limestone face of Rocha da Pena, Nearby the wild peony, Paeonia broterei, is profuse, and its red blooms (photograph page 123) can be seen from February through to May.

encounter the scrub-type vegetation, or *matos*, typical of this region. Outside the Barrocal, the *matos* is very different; some characteristic plants are mentioned on page 120, second paragraph (Walk 22).

Although it ranges over the same botanically rich limestone ridge (now a conservation area) described in earlier editions of the book, we have since changed the original walk, to take into account a newly-waymarked route. This crosses the ridge in a westerly direction and circles back through the village of Penina. Our original route — up to the ridge, eastwards to the ruined windmills and down to the track — was a favourite of many walkers. It is still viable and described above as the Alternative walk. The really energetic can do *both* walks, making a figure of eight!

Start the walk from the **Fonte dos Amoados** (**○**) in **Rocha**, where you park the car. The route to Rocha da Pena is SIGNPOSTED and WAYMARKED (red/yellow) up to the right, on the far side of the café. The ascent is steep for the first few minutes, then the incline lessens, as you enter light woodland. Shown above, an area shaded by carob trees (**P**15; **7min**) enjoys fine views over the farmed countryside. Stay on the track as it swings right, to continue under the cliffs of Rocha da Pena, and slip into a gentler pace to counter the steady ascent. Level stretches give some respite, but the open views to the right are distraction enough to make this section pass quickly. At the top of the hill you reach a CIRCULAR CLEARING (**①**; **21min**).

The onward route up to the trig point on the summit starts here. Look for the waymarked path (signed 'PLAN-ALTO') leaving the clearing immediately to the left of where you entered it, and follow it westwards. *(But for the Alternative walk go straight ahead.)* The well-defined path keeps more or less to the left-hand edge of the ridge top.

The path descends the left-hand edge of a NEOLITHIC

108

STONE WALL which crosses the ridge (**❷**; **31min**). Looking ahead, pick out the cleared area below the final rise to the summit (**42min**). Cross the clearing and walk up a track. The trig point is now over to the left. As the track starts to descend slightly, take the WAYMARKED PATH left up to the TRIG POINT on **Rocha da Pena** (**❸**; **52min**), from where you will have commanding views.

Return from the trig point to the track and turn left to continue. The track now heads down the end of the ridge before curling left towards Penina. As the track descends, *take care;* a section of loose stones underfoot makes walking tricky for a short distance. Once past a minor track running in from the left (**1h 04min**), the track surface improves on the final descent into Penina.

Enter **Penina** (**❹**; **1h11min**) and head downhill into the centre of this typical rural village. In just over a minute, turn left (waymarked) where there is a FOUNTAIN on the upper corner to the right. Take the third village street on the right, to pass a café on the left, then turn left at the T-junction soon reached. Immediately on leaving Penina (**1h 14min**), turn left on a track and, half a minute later, at a three-way junction, turn right on a trail. The trail runs besides a long building on the right, then reverts to path as it skirts a field. In **1h19min** the path emerges on a track, at a bend. (Down to the right is the Penina to Pena road.) Keep ahead on the wide stabilised track now, parallel with Rocha da Pena ridge over to the left. The way undulates through tranquil countryside back to the **Fonte dos Amoados** (**❍**; **1h34min**).

SCRUBLAND is an important type of vegetation in the Mediterranean. But despite many common elements, the scrub is named differently throughout the region. To the east of the Iberian Peninsula, the term *macchie* or *maquis* refers to the tall scrubland, where the shrubs stand about the height of man or more, and *phrygana* or *garrigue* is used for the knee-high, more open scrubland. The Portuguese use one term for both: *matos*; similarly, the Spanish use *mattoral*. The plant communities which make up the *matos* are a good indication of the underlying geology and are especially easy to 'read' in Algarve, to determine whether you are in the Barrocal region or not. The holly oak, *Quercus coccifera* (photograph above), the shrubby wild olive, *Olea europaea*, the wild jasmine, *Jasminium fruticans*, the white small-flowered cistus, *Cistus monspeliensis*, and the dwarf fan palm, *Chamaerops humilis*, are a few of the many plants which reliably indicate the presence of limestone.

Walk 20: SALIR CIRCUIT

Distance: 11km/6.8mi; 2h15min *(allow 3h-3h30min)*

Grade: ● easy-moderate. The walk uses mainly good (although occasionally stony) tracks and paths; there is very little climbing involved.

Equipment: See pages 41-42.

Picnic suggestion: 5min on foot; park on the wide road below Salir

How to get there and return: 🚗 only accessible by car. See details in Car tour 3, page 25. Leave the car on the south side of Salir, near where the N124 bends right to descend towards Loulé (37° 14.406'N, 8° 2.673'W).

Shorter circuit: Salir — Arneiro — Salir (9.2km/5.7mi; 1h50min). ● Grade as main walk. Follow the main walk to where the Algarve Way leaves the road (**❸**). Keep to the Algarve Way. Meet the main road 12 minutes later and cross onto a track signposted 'Pedras Ruivas' (**❻**). Pick up the main walk again at the 1h21min-point.

Even within the confines of the large valley around Salir, there is an unexpected variety in the landscape that can only be appreciated if you are on foot. This walk follows some narrow footpaths, bounded by groves, and broad tracks through wilder regions; it crosses rivers on stepping stones and visits intimate farming communities. We return to the church in the centre of Salir; this is a spectacular viewpoint with an adjacent café/bar and picnic area. We also visit the old castle area shown overleaf, before heading back to the car.

Start the walk at the PARKING PLACE in **Salir** (**❍**): continue to the right and head down the LOULÉ ROAD towards the river and the bridge (PONTE DE SALIR). In **8min**, just before the bridge, turn left on a track (**❶**).* If you encounter a chain-link fence across the track, undo it by using a hook by the wall and put the hook back. As you approach a farm four minutes later, head first for the entrance to the farmyard, then swing left to take a path through olive and carob groves. The path follows a LINE OF POSTS carrying a cable. Ignore paths right and left.

You pass in front of a small house on the left and an OLD BRICK OVEN on the right (**16min**). Immediately after, turn right into a walled trail. At a crossing of trails turn left, and turn left again at a T-junction of trails. Stay ahead, to meet a track by the entrance to a house down to the left (**19min**). Turn right here. In a minute you reach a narrow road at a T-junction (**❷**; **20min**): turn right to continue. As you ascend gently, keep an eye on the roadside vegetation: you might spot the peony, *Paeonia broteroi*,

*If you encounter any problems between the 8min- and 20min-points, note that the wide road joining from the left at the 8min-point (**❶**) leads up to a narrow road (after 0.5km). A right turn on the narrow road would take you past the cemetery on the right and in four minutes you would join the walk at the 20min-point (**❷**).

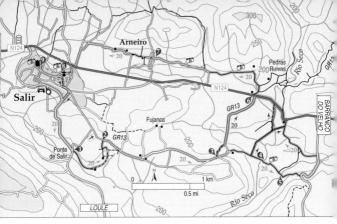

which graces the early months with its elegant red flowers (photograph page 123).

As you reach the top of the rise (**25min**), turn left towards 'FUJANCA'. (Note the stone cross on the wall of the house on the right here.) Then turn right just past the house, on a track (joining the **Algarve Way**). This track runs through orange and almond groves. Pass a track off left, then meet a road on a bend (**30min**); keep straight on here, still on the Algarve Way. Some 600m/yds along, the Algarve Way turns off left — a SHORT-CUT (**3**) back to the road: *take this turning if you are doing the Shorter circuit.* Then the road bends left and starts into a deeper descent (**47min**). Just past this point, two tracks (surfaced initially) join from the right. Ignore the first (with a plaque 'Fonte Morena'); take the *second* track. (*Or keep straight ahead on the road, if you are doing the Shorter circuit and missed the Algarve Way short-cut.*) The track descends gradually through farmland; keep ahead as the main track goes left (**49min**).

The first of TWO RIVERS (**4**) is met in **52min** (*see 'Note' at the*

Note: At some times of year, it may be difficult to cross the Rio Seco (**4**). If so, return to the 49min-point and go right along the track. In three minutes, cross a stream on stepping stones and in a further four minutes cross the Rio Seco on stepping stones. (Or, if the Seco is too deep here as well, refer to the next paragraph.) The white house at the 1h15min-point in the walk is ahead to the left; the track passes behind it, then joins the road.

If the Rio Seco is too deep on this detour route, go along the grassy track on the west side of the river, before you cross it. Follow this to a field, which you skirt to the right. Then descend a steep path back to the river and walk alongside it, to rejoin the main walk along the road. A left turn soon leads to the 1h21min-point (**6**).

111

right), and there are just enough stones for you to step across to continue along the track opposite. This leads to a much STONIER RIVER (**5**), reached four minutes later. Cross this one by heading diagonally right, and join a walled-in track which climbs up and around to the left, affording views back down over the river before the SURFACED ROAD is reached in **1h**.

Turn left down the road, cross the bridge five minutes later, and take a track off left almost immediately. The track leads at first through once-cultivated land, now reverting to *matos*. After crossing a small stream bed (**1h11min**), the track leads diagonally left; then it swings to the right, towards the road and a white house. (The alternative track, used when the Rio Seco is high, enters from the left here; see 'Note' in the panel on page 111) Pass in front of the house to reach the SALIR ROAD (**1h15min**). Turn left downhill along the road and cross the bridge over the **Rio Seco**. (The second 'high water' option joins the road here from the left.) Some 350m/yds past the bridge, just before a house and farm, turn sharp right on a track signposted 'PEDRAS RUIVAS' (**6**; **1h21min**); there is also a sign for the GR13. *(The Shorter circuit rejoins here.)* After only a minute fork left, then fork left again (**1h23min**), before rising uphill through the cork oaks. The track swings left below a square white house and shortly gives you the first views of the white tower by the church in Salir. Descend to meet a narrow road and turn right.

There is a different character to the walk now, as you weave your way back to Salir through a succession of hamlets, taking a course roughly parallel with the main road below left. Stay ahead to enjoy views over the picturesque valley on your left — and Rocha da Pena (Walk 19) slightly to the right. Eventually you reach the hamlet of **Arneiro** (**7**; **1h43min**). At the junction, go ahead up a steep concrete trail between houses. When you meet a road on a bend, follow it straight ahead and into a field track (**1h44min**). This track swings down left; keep ahead here, on a path (alongside a building on the left). When the path joins another field track (**1h46min**), keep ahead. Stay right at the fork and soon meet a concrete road. Turn right to continue through a farmyard. Continue along the concrete road as it dips and rises, to pass through another farmyard. At a T-junction (**1h55min**), turn left towards Salir and soon bend right to another T-junction Then turn left again to head directly towards Salir.

As you join the MAIN N124 ROAD (**1h58min**), turn

Typical Algarvian chimney in Salir

right and then immediately left, up the road signposted to
'SALIR' and 'CASTELO'. Turn right just a minute later, to
follow a surfaced track up towards a higher road
(**2h01min**), where you turn right and then left shortly
afterwards. You come to the CHURCH and SQUARE on the
pinnacle of the hill (**❽**; **2h05min**). There is a superb
panorama from this viewpoint, which you can enjoy from
a seat in the shade — perhaps with a drink from the café.
Nearby is a small PARK area with seating (Picnic 16). But
don't picnic here before midday: while the chimes of the
church clock are pleasing from a distance, close by they are
deafening!

Leave the square the way you entered it* and continue
ahead (passing the road by which you arrived) through old
Salir, to find the remains of the CASTLE. Brown 'CASTELO'
signs lead you to a cobbled street on the right (**2h09min**;
see photograph above), and up to the old RAMPARTS (**❾**).
You can walk along them by swinging right and
continuing around to the left, to complete a circle taking
just four minutes, bringing you back to the 2h09min-
point, but this time facing the church. Head straight down
the street opposite, then fork right, left and left again —
to follow the N124 four 100-150m, back to the PARKING
PLACE (**⊙**; **2h15min**).

*Or, for a speedy return to your car, leave the square down the steps at
the side of the park. Turn left along the village street, then follow it as it
bends right to the Loulé road near the start of the walk.

See also photograph page 23

Distance: 14km/8.7m; 3h15min *(allow about 5h)*

Grade: ● moderate — mainly on good tracks and paths, with occasional stony and difficult sections. The longest climb is to the top of Guilhim at 313m/1026ft.

Equipment: See pages 41-42.

How to get there and return: 🚗 car or 🚌 bus from Faro to/from Estói (journey time 20min). *Warning*: not all buses go into Estói — be sure to refer to Timetable 6, but in any case it is easiest to start the walk by alighting at the Roman Villa at the Milreu crossroads (where the bus turns right to go into Estói before coming out again the same way). Travelling by car, see Car tour 3, page 22 and park in Estói (37° 5.634'N, 7° 53.722'W).or at Milreu (37° 5.681'N, 7° 54.248'W).

Shorter walks: (● all are moderate)

1 Milreu — Guilhim — Milreu (6.9m/4.3mi; 1h52min). 🚌 or 🚗 to Milreu. Follow the main walk from the 14min-point (**1**) to the obelisk on the top of Guilhim (**5**) and the road below (**6**; the 1h13min-point in the main walk). Go right here and stay on this road, passing an old windmill (the diversion to inspect it adds 0.8km/0.5mi). Ignore the track joining from the right two minutes later (where Shorter walk 2 joins). You meet the intersection with your outward route 11 minutes later (**3**; the 34min-point in the main walk). Turn left into the trail, to continue back to Milreu.

2 Milreu — Guilhim — Milreu (7.2km/4.5mi; 1h40min). 🚌 or 🚗 to Milreu. Follow the main walk from the 14min-point (**1**) to the obelisk on the top of Guilhim (**5**) and return the same way, until you reach the end of the track first encountered at the 1h-point in the main walk (**4**). Turn left downhill here, then turn sharp right on meeting a road seven minutes later. Stay ahead and come back to the intersection with your outward route 11 minutes later (**3**; the 34min-point in the main walk). Turn left into the trail, to continue back to Milreu.

3 Milreu — Guilhim — Milreu (9.3km/6.1mi; 2h08min). 🚌 or 🚗 to Milreu. Follow the main walk from the 14min-point (**1**) to the Bordeira road (**7**; the 1h45min-point in the main walk). Then, instead of crossing the bridge, follow the track straight ahead. This leads (in 20 minutes) back to the 26min-point in the main walk (**2**). Turn left here, to continue back to Milreu. (This short-cut passes a quarry, where it can be very dusty for about five minutes, if a lorry passes.)

4 Estói — Guilhim — Fialho (10.9km/6.9mi; 2h26min). Follow the main walk from Estói (**O**) to the Faro road at Fialho (**9**; 2h26min), where you can catch a bus.

5 Estói — Fialho — Estói (11.8km/7.3mi; 2h16min). Follow the main walk to the 26min-point (**2**). Turn right at this junction and follow the track past quarry (see 3 above). You join a narrow surfaced road 19 minutes later, where you turn right to cross a bridge (**7**) and meet the Bordeira road in a minute. From here pick up the main walk (at the 1h45min-point).

E stói has two special points of interest, the ruins of a Roman villa (Milreu, open 09.30-12.30 and 14.00-17.00 daily except Mondays) near the start of the walk, and the Palacio do Visconde de Estói at the end. The villa dates back to about the first or second century BC and is

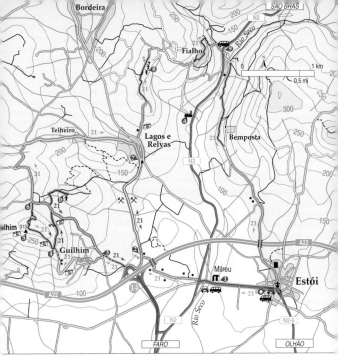

thought to have survived until the eighth century AD. The excavations show a bathing complex still with some mosaic work, as well as foundations of houses and the apse of a Roman temple. The 18th-century palace has been converted into a luxury government *pousada* (open to non-residents for meals, drinks and snacks). Its gardens (photograph page 23; currently undergoing restoration) are curious enough to be interesting.

This walk leaves Estói by the bridge over Rio Seco, to head first for the viewpoint on the summit of Guilhim. Taking a northerly route, a broad ridge is followed for a time. This leads you through areas of cultivation, before you eventually curve around to Fialho and cross the Rio Seco again.

Leave the bus, or park, in **Estói** (**O**). **Start the walk** by heading away from Estói, back towards the main FARO/ SÃO BRÁS ROAD. Visit **Milreu** en route (**❶**; closed Mondays). Cross the main N2 road diagonally (**14min**), into the minor road to the right of the road opposite, and walk straight into rural surroundings where the ubiquitous yellow Bermuda buttercup brightens the way, and where scattered farm houses add interest to this area of cultivation. Keep ahead, eventually bearing right to cross the BRIDGE OVER THE MOTORWAY (**22min**). Once over, descend to a T-junction (**❷**; **26min**) and turn left. (*Shorter* *walks 1, 2 and 3 return to this point, and you turn right here for Shorter walk 5.)* You reach a WELL in about **27min**.

Continue along the minor road, rising above the motorway slip-road down left. About two minutes later, at the top of the rise, turn right to continue on a rough track, heading in the direction of Guilhim. Keep right towards the hill at the fork. The track reverts to path and meets a narrow road (**❸**; **34min**; *Shorter walks 1 and 2 come in from the right here*). Continue left, then right on a narrow road which soon leads through the HAMLET of **Guilhim**.

The views open up to the east — towards Olhão and the mound of São Miguel, easily distinguished by the mast on the top. Reach a cross track (**42min**) and turn right up the rough concrete (to Quinta Lampa). In a few minutes, when the concrete ends at a couple of houses, stay ahead on a field track. The track swings left uphill and continues along the contours, becoming more a trail, then a path. It rises into old olive grove terraces. There are sweeping views left towards the coast before the path heads up to the right (**50min**) and leaves the terraces behind.

You rise onto a track on a bend (**❹**; **1h**). *(Shorter walk 2 returns from the obelisk on Guilhim to this point before heading down the track.)* As you catch a breath here, you can enjoy extensive views — from São Miguel in the east to Faro in the south. Follow the track (for part of the way there is also a path alongside it) up the ridge towards the obelisk. Much of the climbing is over now, and all that

remains is to follow the path through the *matos*, to reach the OBELISK on **Guilhim** (❺; **1h05min**). It is a fantastic look-out point, with views stretching from the coast in the south to the ring of hills in the north.

With your back to the sea, follow the braided track, taking the easy options on this very steep descent. Keep ahead when the track runs into a road at a bend (❻; **1h13min** — *but turn right here for Shorter walk 1*), and continue along the ridge through the cultivated farmlands shown below. At a crossroads after about 600m/yds (**1h20min**), swing sharp right, following the road in a tight U-turn — and now leaving cultivation to head down into the *matos*. When you meet another crossroads 400m/yds further on, turn right. Olive and carob trees provide shade from time to time as you wander down this pleasant country lane to a BRIDGE and the BORDEIRA ROAD (❼; **1h45min**). *(The track ahead before crossing the bridge is used for Shorter walks 3 and 5.)*

Turn left here, in the direction of Bordeira (but note that there is a good café/restaurant to the right). Then take the narrow road on the right just three minutes later. (Or first continue on the main road for another minute, to a café/bakery on the left, from where a path leads up the bank to this narrow road.) Continue as the road rises steeply, giving views of Estói to the right. In **1h55min**, as the tar runs out, the main track swings round and down to the right. Keep straight on along a rough track here,

heading for a villa and a ruined windmill. At a junction of tracks/ trails, follow the main track to the left, to cross over to the far side of the ridge. The track then swings right along the left-hand side of the ridge; you pass two RUINED WIND-MILLS (❽) and a villa on your right and a WATER TANK on the left. The track then becomes surfaced and passes some buildings on the left. You emerge on a road (**2h09min**), where you turn right. Guilhim is now over to the right.

This walk passes through a region dotted with picturesque farms, like the one shown here (about 1h20min into the walk). Citrus fruits, olives, almonds, and carobs are commonly grown. The carob is no longer valued for its crop of beans, which was once used to feed the animals. However, these trees are still abundant throughout the area.

Ignore a turning to the right after 60m/yds but, after another 70m, at a Y-fork, go right downhill (**2h12min**).* Some 170m further on (after the tar has run out), ignore a turning to the left. At the next major junction, after another 300m/yds (and back on tar), take care: the main route swings sharp right, down towards a FACTORY (**a**) on the main road. Turn left here and, after 40m, take the narrow walled-in trail ahead (at the right of a drive to a house). Come to another house (**2h19min**) and skirt it to the left, keeping it to your right. Descend a rough track with two-wheel concrete strips. Ignore tracks off left and right. Go right at a first T-junction, then keep round left to a T-junction with a narrow road (**2h24min**). With a stream bed to your left, continue down to the main FARO/SÃO BRÁS ROAD at **Fialho** (**9**; **2h26min**). *(Those doing Shorter walk 4 can catch a bus back to Faro from here.)*

Cross the road to join a roughly surfaced lane on the far side which leads to a BRIDGE over the **Rio Seco** (**2h29min**). Cross the bridge; ignore turn-offs to the left, but take the first downhill fork to the right (**2h31min**). The track roughly parallels the river, but rises steadily above it. Keep straight ahead when you rise to meet a track on a bend (**2h42min**).

Ignore the track joining from the left (**2h48min**), but when you meet a road on a tight bend just over two minutes later, fork left. Estói comes into view, and soon the way is all descent. The road passes a RETIREMENT HOME (**2h57min**), where you ignore a road to the right. Walking through the intensely-cultivated environs of Estói, you catch glimpses of the old palace. After crossing a BRIDGE OVER THE MOTORWAY, keep ahead at a diagonal crossroads (**3h08min**), with the PALACE GROUNDS to the left. You walk beneath the bridge joining the palace to the formal gardens, then pass the village WASH-HOUSE and FOUNTAIN (both on the left; **3h11min**). Take the first narrow street to the right, just before reaching the small square, and the stepped street to the right 70m further on. This leads to the PALACE GATES and MAIN SQUARE in **Estói** (**o**; **3h 15min**). From here cross over the main road and take the right-hand side street downhill to the BUS SHELTER or your parked car.

*These notes *and measurements* were accurate at press date, but there *are* more (minor) paths in this area than are shown on the map (to show them all would just confuse). If you find yourselves 'off piste', just *head downhill and keep an eye on the factory*. If you come out on the N2 near the factory (**a**), turn left and walk north to regain the route.

Walk 22: SÃO BRÁS • TAREJA • VALE DE ESTACAS • SÃO BRÁS

Distance: 10km/6.2mi; 2h16min *(allow about 4h)*

Grade: ● easy-moderate. There is some climbing involved, through undulating countryside — but nothing excessive (about 250m/820ft overall). The paths and tracks used are stony and difficult in some places.

Equipment: See pages 41-42.

Picnic suggestion: park near the track off left just east of Tareja and walk down to the track to the river and a ruined mill (57min-point in the walk)

How to get there and return: 🚗 car or 🚌 bus from Faro to/from São Brás (Timetable 6). Journey time 35min. Travelling by car, park in the centre *(centro)*, on the wide dual carriageway road (on the route of the walk), leading north from the main square and signposted 'Correios' and 'Mercado Municipal'. It is easier to park near the 9min-point in the walk (37° 9.536'N, 7° 53.356'W). On Saturdays (market day), one carriageway is closed, and the other temporarily reverts to two-way traffic.

Shorter walks: (both are ●)

1 São Brás — Tareja — São Brás (8.6km/5.3mi; 1h45min). Follow the main walk beyond Tareja, to the track met at the 54min-point (**4**). Turn right here (instead of left), and follow the track to a surfaced road near a bridge and a fountain down on the left (Fonte de Tareja; **8**; 1h03min). Turn right now to Tareja (**3**) and retrace your outward route back to the start.

2 São Brás — Tareja — São Brás (8km/5mi; 1h38min). Follow the main walk to the road just below the centre of Tareja (**3**; 36min). Instead of turning left to the centre a minute later, keep ahead along the road, passing the Fonte de Tareja (**8**) on the left. When this road swings up left (44min), stay ahead on a track. At the T of tracks (47min), turn right; three minutes later, turn right again, passing to the left of the well shown on page 121 (Fonte do Bico Alto; **9**). Ahead is Tareja. Follow this track back to the Tareja road and turn left towards Tareja. Retrace the route of the outward walk back to the start.

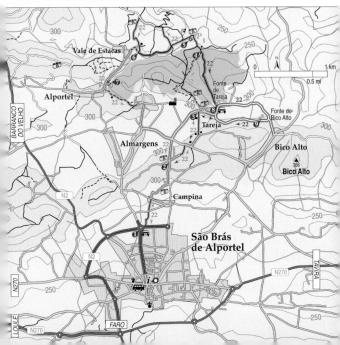

São Brás lies on the edge of the Barrocal, the limestone region. This walk leads through interesting pastoral landscapes to the village of Tareja and continues into a very different region — the schists of the northern *serras*.

Here the acidic soils support a *matos* which is very different from that in the limestone regions. Cistus dominates, particularly the large sticky-leaved *Cistus ladanifer,* which often covers the rolling hills. The large white flowers, sometimes blotched with dark red at the base of the petals, are short-lasting like all cistus and are never produced in sufficient numbers to smother the hillsides in blossom. Cork oaks too are present, as a reminder of an earlier time, when the vegetation consisted largely of oak forest with an undergrowth of cistus. Colour is added by the heaths — the white-flowered tree heather, *Erica lusitanica,* and the pink *Erica australis,* both of which have a prolonged flowering period, and by the dark blue lavender, *Lavandula stoechas.*

Start the walk from the MAIN SQUARE (**O**; with tourist information office) in **São Brás**. (To start from the BUS STATION at **Ⓐ**, turn right out of the station and right again in front of a chapel. Cross over one street and at the next street turn left.) Head up the wide DUAL CARRIAGEWAY road towards 'CORREIOS' and 'MERCADO MUNICIPAL'. In **9min**, at the large ROUNDABOUT (**❶**) in the central reservation just before the end of the dual carriageway, turn right into another dual carriageway and, almost immediately, cross the zebra crossing into a walled-in track.

A steady ascent begins, and the track rises to meet a road. Cross the road to enter a walled-in track which rises to cross another road (**15min**). Still in steady ascent, take the narrow road opposite. This walled-in road continues round to the right into more open countryside. Views to the east here include the mound of São Miguel, with its tall mast.

Keep ahead as the road descends to a junction, by a WELL (**21min**), and turn left up another road, heading towards the brow of a hill. At the brow of the hill (**❷**; **25min**), where a left turn leads to a *miradouro*, turn right on a road which becomes a walled-in track. You meet another road four minutes later, where you turn right. Enter a narrow walled-in road on the left just a minute later, immediately past a building on the left-hand corner. At a fork (**32min**) take the downhill track to the left, between houses. This soon leads behind a building on the left.

Come to a surfaced road (**❸**; **36min**) and turn right. Turn sharp left a minute later into **Tareja**, passing the WASH-HOUSE on the left. *(But keep straight along the road for Shorter walk 2.)* The road leads to a T-junction (**38min**), where you turn left. From here there is a fine view to the north over rolling hills and valleys; it is easy to see the strategic position of the village. Follow the road between

Shorter walk 2 passes this Moorish-style well with a wheel, the Fonte do Bico Alto.

the houses, until it swings right and ends a minute later. Continue on a footpath, climbing towards the ridge ahead, with views of *matos*-covered hillsides on the right and the valley already traversed on the left.

In **40min**, stay ahead on the path, past a THRESHING FLOOR on the left. The path leads towards a small plateau, once another threshing floor, on top of the ridge (**41min**). Carpets of *Romulea bulbocodium* display a variety of shades in their small lilac flowers here. Continue over the hill, to meet the bend of a narrow track which can be seen ahead (**42min**). Keep straight on (right) along this track, to head into the *matos*. Ignore two tracks coming in from the left, and stay ahead as the lesser track you are on narrows to a path (often ploughed over). Descend to the main track — either by going straight ahead or by going downhill to the right at the left of a gully. Quickly meeting the main track, go left (**❹**; **54min**). *(But turn right here for Shorter walk 1.)* Ignore the track that soon comes up on the right. Passing an OLD RUIN on the right, keep right at a track junction, to the RIVER (**P**18; **57min**). The river area is a fine picnic spot, brightened by paper-white narcissi and pink oleander.

Cross the river on stepping stones and follow the track round to the far side of the ruined WATERMILL (**❺**). Rise away from the confluence of rivers, keeping the mill on your left. From the mill continue ahead along the track for about four minutes*, then go right on a rising track, towards a high FENCE. You pass a WATER HOLE in a compound over to the right. When you reach the top, join a track coming in from the left and continue in the same direction. Follow the spine of a ridge through scattered cork oak plantations, ignoring all turn-offs.

Soon after the high point (**1h10min**), the track dips down into a hollow, where a track crosses. Turn left on this track, heading for a cluster of buildings (Vale de Estacas) which can be seen on the road below. You follow a small ridge and then descend its left flank towards a meadow. Keep on the track past a house on the left, and go right downhill at the junction immediately afterwards (**❻**; **1h20min**). *(The track from the mill, mentioned in the footnote below, joins here.)* Cross the river diagonally to the right on stepping stones and continue on a field track back

---

*An alternative is to continue along the track past the mill for 12 minutes, keeping the river over to your left; this leads to the 1h20min-point in the main walk.

ALGARVIAN FLOWERS

Top to bottom: Paeonia broteroi,
Anemone palmata, Narcissus papy-
raceus *(paper-white narcissus)*,
Ophrys fusca, Aceras anthropophorum,
Convolvulus tricolor

to the riverbank, then go left alongside the river on a path. The path widens to a track as it leaves the riverbank. Keep ahead, as a lane joins from the left, and meet the village road at **Vale de Estacas** (**1h24min**).

Turn left, but then leave the road four minutes later (after passing an ELECTRICITY SUB-STATION on the left; ❼), to take a stony path on the left (by a crash barrier). This path slopes down to a stream and more paper-white narcissi. Cross the stream ahead and continue to the right in a gradual ascent. Keep ahead and pass to the left of a white house, from where you stay ahead on the walled-in trail.

Keep left at the point where a track joins from the right (**1h 35min**) and continue along this track. It becomes surfaced and meets another road, where you turn right. Turn right again on another road almost imme-diately. As you rise to another road in a cluster of houses (**1h 40min**), turn left and left again to continue. Ignore the road just to the left; keep ahead to a crossroads (**1h47min**), where you turn right uphill. The road on the left at the top of the rise (❷; **1h51min**) was the 25min-point in your outward route; keep straight on here to retrace your steps to **São Brás** (❶; **2h16min**).

Walk 23: TAVIRA NATIONAL FOREST

Distance: 8.0km/5mi; 1h48min *(allow 2h30min-3h)*

Grade: ● easy-moderate. The walk, mainly on tracks, is fairly easy going, apart from a tricky descent to cross the river towards the end. The only significant climbing is up to the trig point.

Equipment: See pages 41-42.

How to get there and return: ⛐ only accessible by car. Travelling east on the N125 from the Faro area, look for the large Ozadi Hotel, some 3km beyond the bridge at Tavira. Turn left 350m past the road to the hotel, for 'Mata da Conceição' (brown signpost). Swing right in 600m, to cross the bridge over the stream, and continue ahead. Keep left at a junction (2.9km from the main road). Go under the motorway; then park in the open area (4.7km from the main road); a house is up to the left and there is a forest map board (37° 10.674'N, 7° 35.975'W).

Shorter walks (all three are ●)

1 Car parking area — ruins — car parking area (5km/3.1mi; 1h05min). Easy. Follow the main walk through the cutting (❷; 28min). Two minutes later, just before some ruins (❸) on the left, turn right on a path. Follow this path along a winding valley. At a faint fork, go left to cross the stream, to continue with it on your right. Head up the valley, keeping to the right of the woodland. In seven minutes you rise up to a track; cross it and join a track directly opposite. Go down this grassy track. In 17 minutes you reach the outward route at the ford (❶), from where you return to your car.

2 Car parking area — trig point diversion — car parking area (5.7km/3.5mi; 1h30min). Easy-moderate. Follow the main walk to the cutting (❷; 28min), then take the wide track off right immediately beyond it. Continue up this track for six minutes (350m/yds), then cross another track entering from the left. After 100m you rejoin the main walk at the 53min-point (❻): follow it to the end, omitting the ascent to Asseiceira. If you *do* climb to this trig point (❼), add 1km/0.6mi; 20min.

3 Car parking area — Malhada — Daroeira — car parking area (6.5km/4.0mi; 1h21min). Easy. Follow the main walk to the junction at the 53min-point (❻) at the top of the hill. Then turn right instead of left and, a minute later, take the grassy track off left. Within ten minutes this takes you down to the river ford (❶) first reached at the 17min-point in the main walk. From here retrace your steps back to the car.

The Mata da Conceição is not the grand forest region that its name suggests, but merely a fairly large plantation of eucalyptus trees. Our walk quickly takes you through the forest and into the pleasing countryside beyond it. The *matos*-covered hills hiding small villages seem to roll timelessly away, creating an extremely photogenic landscape, given a clear day and a touch of colour in the countryside.

Start out from the CAR PARKING AREA (❍) at the **Mata da Conceição**: continue northeast along the surfaced road. After **3min** (280m/yds) turn left on a surfaced road towards 'MALHADA DO PERES'. Stay ahead on a track as the road swings off right (**4min**). Keep ahead at the junction of tracks reached after another 250m (**7min**).

View to Malhada from the cutting reached in 28min

Now in gentle descent, the track soon winds down to a T-junction (*a left turn here leads to a pleasant riverside picnic spot in two minutes*). Turn *right* here, to a ford over the **Ribeira da Gafa** (**❶**; **17min**). Cross over and continue on the track beyond *(the return route for Short walks 1 and 3 is the field track on the right here)*. Follow the main track up from the river, leaving the forest behind, to enjoy more open views. Look up to the right now, to see the trig point on top of Asseiceira; it is almost hidden by a villa. *Take note of this now*, because the villa obscures it completely later in the walk.

There is some climbing involved now, until you reach a CUTTING (**❷**; **28min**). Beyond here you get your first real taste of the panoramic views which can be enjoyed throughout much of the rest of the walk. Ignore the track off right just beyond the cutting *(but turn right here for Short walk 2)*. The village of Malhada can be seen below to the left. The track leads past some RUINS (**❸**) on the left

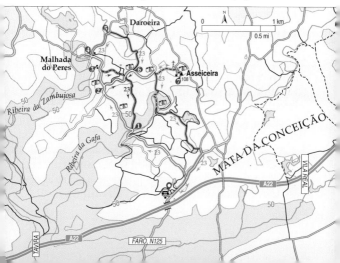

two minutes later. *(Short walk 1 leaves the main walk just before these ruins, along the path to the right.)* At a road junction on the edge of **Malhada do Peres** (**❹**; **35min**), take the second right turn, passing the remains of a round hut *(palheiro)* on the right. Head towards the village of Daroeira, which soon comes into view. Cross the **Ribeira da Zambujosa** (**❺**; **40min**), then turn right on a track a minute later. **Daroeira** is close by on the left now, but it is soon left behind, when you bear right at the next junction (**44min**). A brief ascent here sees you climbing above the Zambujosa, which is now on the right, only to descend to re-cross it (**47min**).

The walk takes on a different pastoral ambience for a time, as you climb steeply away from the river. Looking back as you ascend, there are some fine views over Daroeira. Turn left when you meet another track at the top of the hill (**❻**; **53min**. *(But go right for Short walk 3.)* You enjoy more good views from this high level track. As you near the trig point (obscured by the villa), turn right (**59min**) on a rough track descending between two CAROB TREES. The diversion to the trig point starts as you reach these carobs. From here descend the narrow gully to the left, in the direction of the trig point, taking great care over the stony ground. From the bottom of the gully, head up to the trig point, taking the line between the *matos* on the right and the almond grove on the left. Nearing the villa, head for the PYLON. You come onto a driveway: follow it to within 20m of the villa, then find the ongoing path through thick matos. From the TRIG POINT on **Asseiceira** (108m/355ft; **❼**; **1h09min**) there is a fine panorama.

Return to the two carob trees by the side of the track, then turn left down the stony track towards the valley. Keep to this main track, staying left along a saddle (**1h 23min**). Your onward track can be seen to the right, on the far side of the river. Leave the saddle in the dip, by taking a strong path down to the right, towards a field below. Walk across the field to the right, heading towards the river, reached four minutes later. Go left along the riverbank, to descend to water level. Cross the river on stepping stones, then rise up half-right to the hairpin bend of a track, where you turn left. Follow this back up into the forest, keeping right at the next fork, 200m further on. Keep right at the next two forks, then left at a further three, to eventually join a surfaced road (**1h40min**). Turn right here, then turn right again at a junction. This road leads back to the CAR PARKING AREA (**❍**; **1h48min**).

Walk 24: CASTRO MARIM NATURE RESERVE

Distance: 9.8km/6.1mi; 1h45min *(allow about 3h), plus 15 minutes on foot from the train station or 25 minutes from the bus stop*

Grade: ● easy, but this walk is virtually flat, which can be very tiring over a long distance.

Equipment: See pages 41-42.

How to get there and return: 🚗 car, 🚌 bus (ⓑ; Timetable 8) or 🚂 train (Timetable 9) from Faro to/from Vila Real de Santo António. Journey time by bus 1h40min. Journey time by train, depending on the number of stops, from 1h18min to 1h44min. From the train station (ⓒ) it's only 1.6km/1mi to the start of the walk (go down the station approach past a bar, and at the second bar turn right along a side street which comes out on the main road leading back across the railway to the nature reserve). Travelling by car, note that Castro Marim lies just to the northwest of Vila Real; see Car tour 4 (page 30) for details of how to get there. Park by a ruined building down the track to the left, some 1.6km/1mi after turning north onto the N122 from the main N125 immediately outside Vila Real (37° 12.282'N, 7° 26.134'W). *Note:* this is the *second* track to the left with a ruin, 200m north of the first track left (ⓐ; see map). *To return*: Walk to Castro Marim and, from there, return by taxi for your bus or train (Timetables 8, 9) from Vila Real to Faro.

Some 20 minutes into the walk you can see familiar farmland crops just a short distance away — very different from the vegetation growing close to the salinas, *where only salt-tolerant plants like the glassworts* (Arthrocnemem sp) *and the saltworts* (Salicornia sp) *can survive.*

Although the walk starts just to the south of Castro Marim, it is well worth having a look around the town — either before you start out or at the end of the walk. If you are travelling by public transport, save this until the end of the walk, so that you can take a taxi back from there to Vila Real. A castle and a 17th-century fort dominate the town. The castle is believed to have its origins back in Roman times, but was the seat of the Knights of Christ in the 14th century until this was transferred to Tomar. The earthquake of 1755 largely destroyed the castle, although parts still remain, and the present castle was built by King Afonso III. You can stroll around inside to inspect the old walls and enjoy its commanding location, looking over the Rio Guadiana towards Ayamonte in Spain.

The nature reserve itself covers the area of *salinas* south and east of the town. *Salinas* are the production units used to obtain sea salt. They are flooded with sea water which is allowed to evaporate under the influence of the sun and the strong coastal winds, until the salt finally crystallises out. With its long hot summers, Algarve is an ideal location for salt production by this method, and its history dates back more than 2500 years, from the time when salt was first produced for preserving fish. Castro Marim was a particu-

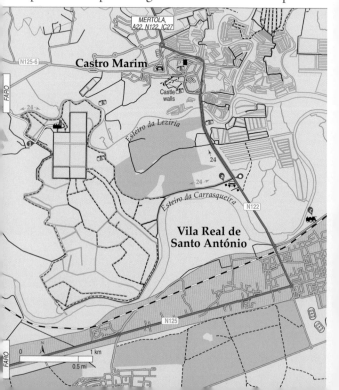

larly important centre for this activity, and today there are over 300 hectares (350 square miles) of these 'salt gardens' spread between Castro Marim and Vila Real.

They are valuable sites for wild life, especially wading birds and waterfowl. This walk will delight the bird-watchers particularly, and the birds that you can expect to see, depending on the season, include flamingos, *Phoenicopterus ruber*, in a large flock, the lovely black-winged stilt, *Himantopus himantopus*, which is the symbol of this reserve, the white stork, *Ciconia ciconia*, and a variety of other birds which we are not skilled enough to identify. The list of known visitors to the reserve is too long to quote in full, but includes a number of sandpipers such as the dunlin, *Calidris alpina,* plovers like the ringed plover, *Charadrius hiaticula*, and the avocet, *Recurvirostra avosetta*.

In the past walkers were free to wander throughout the reserve area, but a few years ago access was restricted to protect the environment. *Only three routes in the reserve are open to the public; the best is the one described below.* But if you would like to try another, go to www.icnf.pt/portal/turnatur/visit-ap/rn/rnscmvrsa. You should be able to click on the three 'PR' routes (walks) and at least see a sketch map showing the location. Unfortunately the website is

only in Portuguese, but if you google 'Reserva Natural do Sapal de Castro Marim', you'll find quite a bit of information in English. It's the oldest nature reserve in Portugal.

Start the walk from the N122 just south of **Castro Marim** (22 minutes' walking from the centre) and 1.6km/1mi north of the N125. Take the track heading west (**❍**), where cultivation south of Castro Marim ends. A ruined building on the left is passed in **3min** (**❶**), as you head out towards the *salinas.* From here the river over to the left becomes more noticeable. Olive and carob groves on the right add colour and contrast to the flatness of the *salinas* now on the left. The flamingos are usually in a large flock, so they are easily seen across the emptiness of the large lagoons.

Stay with the main track, as you

The flock of flamingos is often seen at these large salinas near the start of the walk. If they are too frequently disturbed by visitors, they move to the quieter western parts of the reserve.

swing around right, to get good views of Castro Marim. The closest point to the castle is reached in **24min**, as you swing left on meeting the river. Keep following the main track, with an eye open for the wading birds in some of the shallower parts of the reserve. As the sun gets stronger the storks take to the wing, and they can be seen lazily circling and rising on the thermals.

After reaching the SALT PLANT (❶; **42min**) and taking a break, retrace steps to the N122 (◯; **1h45min**).

In Tavira

BUS AND TRAIN TIMETABLES

Eva Transportes (www.eva-bus.com) operates local buses all over Algarve as well as servicing long distance routes to Lisbon, Porto and other major towns in Portugal. Its yellow, green and blue logo and the word Eva, is used to mark its buses and bus stops. Frota Azul (www.frotazul-algarve.pt) operates services out of Portimão to Monchique and a joint service with Eva to Silves. Printed timetables often can be obtained at the main bus stations and tourist information offices, where timetables are also posted.

A keen bus user has written to praise an *unofficial* website run by a resident: 'www.algarvebus.info is more accurate than individual company websites and better than relying on the availability of printed timetables or information at bus stations. Return tickets are often the same price as singles and only available from bus stations rather than drivers. There are excellent value bus passes for tourists valid for 3 or 7 days (which must be consecutive). They are useful for walks as they are valid on country buses run by both companies but not on city buses, airport buses or express buses. Buses can get very crowded on schooldays between 8am and 9am and also between 4.30pm and 5pm.'

Remember that bus timetables are liable to change without notice, so always be sure to check the times of your bus. Do not rely solely on the timetables printed on the following pages. Buses are not numbered, but the final destination is displayed on the front, so check before you board.

For some bus journeys it is necessary to book a ticket before you board, particularly when you board at a bus station; for others you pay on the bus. On some journeys there is a 15% discount if you book a return ticket. If you are setting out on a long-distance journey, it is normal to book in advance. If your accommodation is not near a bus station, you can book through a nearby travel agency. The tourist office will advise you of the nearest.

In the list below, the numbers following place names refer to **bus timetable numbers** (except for 9, which is a **train timetable**). The train is considerably cheaper than the bus but, be warned, it is often much slower.

Albufeira 5, 7, 9	Faro 6, 8, 9	Portimão 3, 4, 9
Albufeira station 9	Figueira 2	Sagres 2
Armação de Pera 11	Lagôa 4, 9	Salema 2
Benagil/Marinha 10	Lagos 1, 2, 9	São Brás de Alportel 6
Burgau 1	Luz 1	Silves 4, 5, 9
Caldas de Monchique 3	Monchique 3	Tavira 8, 9
Estói 6	Paderne 7	Vila Real de S A 8, 9

Timetables begin on the next page.

1 Lagos — Luz — Burgau (www.aonda.pt)
Daily departures
Journey times: Lagos — Luz 15min; Lagos — Burgau 22min
Departs Lagos 07.58; 08.43; 09.28; 10.13; 10.58; 12.03; 12.28; 13.38; 13.58; 15.28; 16.13; 17.58
Departs Burgau 08.39; 09.24; 10.14; 11.39; 12.49; 13.14; 14.39; 16.14

2 Lagos — Salema — Figueira — Sagres (www.eva-bus.com)
Daily departures
Journey times: Lagos — Salema 32min, Lagos — Sagres 55min
Departs Lagos 07.15a; 09.15, 10.30c; 10.45; 12.40; 13.35a; 15.10; 16.30; 17.30c; 18.00d; 18.30c; 19.40c; 20.30
Departs Sagres 07.15; 07.40, 08.10a; 10.25, 12.05; 13.40, 15.15c; 15.20c; 16.15; 17.25c; 18.30c; 19.35c
a = except Sun-/holidays; b = Sun-/holidays only; c = Mon-Fri only;
d = Sat, Sun and holidays only

3 Portimão — Monchique (www.frotazul-algarve.pt)
Daily departure times

Portimão (depart)	07.50c, 09.00, 10.00c, 11.10, 13.45c, 14.15, 17.15c, 18.30, 20.30
Caldas de Monchique*	08.13c, 09.23, 10.23c, 11.33, 14.08c, 14.38, 17.38c, 18.53, 20.53
Monchique (arrive)	08.43c, 09.32, 10.32c, 11.50, 00.00, 15.00, 18.00c, 19.15, 21.15
Monchique (depart)	07.00, 08.00, 08.45c, 10.00, 12.30, 14.00c, 14.30d, 15.30c, 18.15
Portimão (arrive)	07.45, 08.45, 09.30, 10.45, 13.15, 14.45, 15.15, 16.15, 19.00

00.00 = does not call
a = except Sun-/holidays; b = Sun-/holidays only; c = Mon-Fri only;
d = Sat, Sun and holidays only
*The bus stops on the main road above Caldas, leaving a short walk down to the village

4 Portimão — Lagôa — Silves (www.frotazul-algarve.pt)
Daily departures
Journey time Portimão — Lagôa 20min, Portimão — Silves 35min
Departs Portimão 07.30c; 08.30; 10.45a: 12.00; 14.15c; 15.50; 16.30c; 17.45; 19.10
Departs Silves 07.15c; 07.40; 09.00; 10.25c; 11.05; 13.05c; 13.50 (Sat only); 15.00; 16.30c; 18.10
a = except Sun-/holidays; b = Sun-/holidays only; c = Mon-Fri only;
d = Sat, Sun and holidays only

5 Albufeira — Silves (www.eva-bus.com)
Daily departures
Journey time Albufeira — Silves 42min
Departs Albufeira 07.20c; 08.05; 09.45a; 12.35; 14.15c; 17.40a; 19.15
Departs Silves 06.40; 07.20c; 08.05a; 10.15; 13.35a; 16.50c; 18.25
a = except Sun-/holidays; b = Sun-/holidays only; c = Mon-Fri only;
d = Sat, Sun and holidays only

Faro — Estói — São Brás (www.eva-bus.com)

Departure times (weekdays)

Faro	Estói	São Brás de Alportel arrive	depart	Estói	Faro
07.45	08.05	08.20	07.00	07.21	07.42
09.00	09.15a	09.27	07.10	07.20a	07.38
10.15	10.35	10.50	00.00	07.25	07.43
12.10	12.36	12.50	08.15	08.25a	08.43
12.35	12.57	00.00	08.25	08.25	08.47
13.35	13.55	14.10	09.50	10.05	10.25
16.30	16.50	17.05	12.35	12.50	13.10
17.30	17.48	17.58	00.00	13.00	13.22
18.25	18.47	19.08	00.00	13.30	13.48
18.30	18.50	19.05	14.15	14.30	14.50
18.40	18.58	00.00	15.20	15.35	15.55
19.15	19.37	00.00	17.30	17.45	18.05
19.20	19.39a	19.50	00.00	18.15	18.35
			18.45	19.00	19.20

Departure times (weekends)

Faro	Estói	São Brás de Alportel		Estói	Faro
07.45b	08.05b	08.20	00.00	07.25	07.45
09.00	09.25	09.27	07.10	07.26a	07.45
12.35	12.51	13.06	09.50c	10.05b	10.25
13.35	13.57	14.10	00.00	13.00a	13.22
16.30	16.50	17.05	14.15b	14.30	14.50
18.25	18.47	19.08	17.30	17.45	18.05
19.20	19.39a	19.50	19.30c	19.40a	20.05

a = bus does not enter Estói, but stops at the crossroads about 1km away —
   convenient both for visiting the Roman ruins (Milreu) and for Walk 21
b = Saturdays only
c = Sundays only
00.00 = does not call

Albufeira — Paderne (www.eva-bus.com)

Daily departures
Journey time Albufeira — Paderne 21min
Departs Albufeira 10.00 (Mon and Fri only); 12.35c; 13.40; 16.15c;
   17.40a; 18.35; 19.30
Departs Paderne 07.05; 08.06; 09.40c; 10.45 (Mon and Fri only); 14.30
   (Mon only); 16.50 (Sat only); 17.55c; 18.25c
a = except Sun-/holidays; b = Sun-/holidays only; c = Mon-Fri only; d = Sat,
   Sun and holidays only

Faro — Tavira — Vila Real de Santo António
(www.eva-bus.com)
Daily departures
Journey times: Faro — Tavira 1h, Faro — Vila Real 1h40min
Departs Faro 07.15; 08.00c; 09.00; 11.00; 12.15c; 13.25, 15.15;
   16.35c; 17.40c; 18.20; 19.30
Departs Vila Real 07.00; 08.15a; 10.00c; 11.20; 12.15; 14.30; 16.30;
   17.30c; 18.30
a = except Sun-/holidays; b = Sun-/holidays only; c = Mon-Fri only;
d = Sat, Sun and holidays only

9   Train timetable, Lagos — Vila Real

This is an extract from the full timetable which is available fre
of charge from most railway stations and some tourist offices. Full details ar
given at the website www.cp.pt, but the site is only in Portuguese at presen
All the train departures are listed below, but only a selection of stations
included. *Note that over-65s can get a 50% discount on fares on production of
passport as proof of age.*

Lagos	Portimão	Silves	Albufeira	Faro	Tavira	V Rea
00.00	00.00	00.00	05.21	06.15	07.05	07.4
00.00	00.00	00.00	07.03	08.00	08.52	09.3
06.10	06.40	06.59	07.47	08.30	00.00	00.0
07.15	07.31	07.45	08.16	08.55	09.29	09.5
07.55	08.29	08.48	09.23	10.10	00.00	00.0
09.33	09.57	10.13	10.46	00.00	00.00	00.0
00.00	00.00	00.00	00.00	10.15	11.04	11.4
00.00	00.00	00.00	00.00	12.12	13.00	00.0
00.00	00.00	00.00	12.31	13.02	13.38	14.0
12.15	12.33	12.49	13.19	00.00	00.00	00.0
13.30	13.52	14.14	00.00	00.00	00.00	00.0
00.00	00.00	00.00	15.03	16.03	16.50	17.4
14.15	14.48	15.09	15.49	16.45	00.00	00.0
18.20	18.36	18.50	19.25	19.56	20.30	20.5
19.12	19.42	20.06	20.49	21.35	22.17	22.5

V Real	Tavira	Faro	Albufeira	Silves	Portimão	Lago
05.30	06.03	06.45	07.27	08.12	08.30	08.5
06.35	07.09	07.52	08.33	00.00	00.00	00.0
07.50	08.17	08.57	09.24	09.47	09.59	10.1
08.55	09.31	10.25	11.11	12.09	12.32	12.5
10.20	11.05	11.51	00.00	00.00	00.00	00.0
00.00	00.00	12.20	13.18	13.55	14.19	14.4
12.40	13.07	13.46	00.00	00.00	00.00	00.0
14.20	15.00	15.53	16.49	00.00	00.00	00.0
16.15	16.49	17.30	17.57	00.00	00.00	00.0
00.00	00.00	17.45	18.38	19.19	19.40	20.0
16.55	17.43	18.35	00.00	00.00	00.00	00.0
17.55	18.26	19.06	19.40	20.08	20.16	20.3
19.05	19.54	20.50	21.36	00.00	00.00	00.0
21.40	22.16	23.00	23.35			

00.00 = does not call

10 Lagôa — Benagil; Lagôa — Praia da Marinha

Daily departures from Lagôa, journey time 15 minutes; NO return buses
Departs for Benagil 9.25, 15.00; Departs for Praia da Marinha 08.50, 14.

11 Lagôa — Armação de Pera

Daily departures from Lagôa, journey time 10-25 minutes
Departs for Armação de Pera 07.45, 08.35, 09.20, 10.40, 11.20, 13.00
   15.20, 16.20, 17.20, 18.30, 19.30
Departs for Lagôa 07.10, 07.55, 08.55, 09.05, 09.30, 10.25, 10.50, 12.
   13.50, 14.00, 14.35, 15.15, 15.50, 16.35, 17.45, 18.00, 18.20, 18.4
   19.00, 19.35, 20.55

Index

Geographical names comprise the only entries in this index. For subject entries, see Contents, page 3. *Italic type* indicates a map reference; **bold face type** a photograph. Both of these may be in addition to a text reference on the same page.